*A Love That Stood The Test of Time*

I0620455

# THE WAY IT WAS
## WITH
## *Gracie*

## ALVIN FUHRMAN

# *About the Book*

Based on his very own life tale, *The Way It Was with Gracie: A Love That Stood The Test of Time* is a touching narrative by Alvin Fuhrman that tries to encapsulate the enduring love story between him and his cherished wife Gracie. This genuine story takes readers on a emotional cruise from that unforgettable day at a bustling farmers market in 1949 up to the last precious breaths of Gracie with Alvin on her bedside, holding her hand.

With their heartfelt letters exchanged throughout Alvin's time in the military, the hardships of long-distance love, and the simple but priceless delights of their life together, this memoir provides an up-close appreciation of what makes love last a lifetime.

# *About the Author*

As a devoted family man Alvin Fuhrman stands out as a major figure in telecommunications with over seven decades of professional experience. Alvin Fuhrman started his career path in 1949 when he assisted in saving the Muenster Telephone Company during ice storms with his brother Bill by his side. After his two-year military service in Germany with the 2nd Armored Division Alvin returned home to work as the only repairman for the company and grew its client base to over 10,000 accounts. Through his dedication to community service he achieved major technological progress and established local programs which included creating the Germanfest. After spending 63 years as Gracie's husband and father to Gene whose death had a profound effect on him, Alvin's life demonstrates strong endurance and the unbreakable ties of family relationships.

Alvin Fuhrman writes with heartfelt dedication as a true storyteller who seeks to depict life's most precious moments. *The Way It Was* served as his debut memoir where readers first encountered his distinctive storytelling style and emotionally resonant stories.

Through *The Way It Was with Gracie: A Love That Stood The Test of Time*, Alvin explores his personal experiences while recounting the remarkable relationship he shared with his deceased wife

Gracie. Alvin's powerful narration captures their romantic journey through seventy-five years of shared experiences while celebrating the devotion and resilience that characterized their bond.

# *Introduction*

T he decision to write *The Way It Was with Gracie: A Love That Stood The Test of Time* stemmed from my need to pay tribute to seventy-five years of extraordinary love with my wife Gracie. When she passed away I knew an important chapter had closed which led me to think about our remarkable shared life.

Gracie was my trusted friend and life partner while also being the one person I loved the most. At a lively farmers market in 1949, our story started when a quiet spark ignited between us. That initial moment of connection transformed into a flame which illuminated our lives for decades filled with happiness, obstacles, and numerous treasured memories. This book allows me to share our story while providing insight into the profound connection between us and a timeless love that transcends boundaries.

# *Dedication*

To Gracie,

Your unyielding strength combined with limitless love and gentle spirit transformed our family life beyond what language can describe. While I move forward through life's pages without you, I carry your spirit in every cherished moment. Through your kindness and endurance, you showed me how to live life with an open heart and to find joy even when grief surrounds me. The book stands as proof of your everlasting influence and honors the love that will forever connect us.

With all my love,
Alvin

*Chapter One*

# Last Moments with Gracie

The home hospice turned the living room into a space for quiet reflection by placing a hospital bed in its center. The lively room that once echoed with laughter and conversation now stood as a silent witness to the last chapter of our shared journey with my beloved.

Choosing home hospice care creates a mix of emotions. A loved one can experience their final days at home in an environment filled with familiar memories and family support. Your home environment becomes a vivid symbol of life's vulnerability through this transformation.

The decline of Gracie's health started with a tragic fall during the pandemic which was part of a gradual deterioration over time.

Gracie had always been a fighter. She approached the difficulties following her hip replacement with determination. Gracie faced the grueling hospital days with determination which demonstrated her resilience at each stage.

Gracie would arrive dressed and prepared for work each morning before her accident when she went down to the telephone office. At that time she had a few responsibilities at work so she occupied herself by sitting at her computer desk every day. When the virus hit, everything changed. The office closure disrupted Gracie's daily routine. She showed determination to return to her routine each day regardless of her situation. However, she was told that she couldn't. She stayed in her lounge chair appearing as a mere reflection of her past self. Every time I passed her on my way to either the utility room or the bathroom I would stop and give her a kiss. She replied with a smile "Oh, that was good," and we both cherished these moments by savoring the small comforts. We kept our spirits playful even though we felt exhausted. Our interactions were full of light-hearted teasing where I would say "Tonight, we'll do it," but our exhaustion prevented us from ever acting on these playful propositions nevertheless our banter sustained our bond.

Gracie got up during the night yet again. The women assigned to watch Gracie didn't allow her to get up, but she used her walker softly to move around by herself. During an unfortunate moment she lost her balance which led to a fall that broke her hip. Her gradual decline began at this point, progressing slowly into a heartbreaking journey that ultimately led us to this critical juncture. Gracie's strength and spirit stayed with us through her health's decline. Our relationship stayed strong because of our love and humor while each kiss we shared reinforced our bond.

I observed her eyes clear suddenly on the second day in the hospice, which then sparkled with peace that extended over her entire face. With each passing day in the hospice I began to remember our remarkable shared journey. We adapted to unexpected changes during the virus outbreak which strengthened our connection to each other. The pandemic enforced physical separation between us while our emotional bond deepened. We discovered fresh methods for communication that allowed us to share our love and support with each other.

I spent those extended silent days sitting next to Gracie's bed while reflecting on the shared life we created together. The day we met at the farmers market in 1949 emerged in my mind more vividly than any other memory from that time. The market stalls displayed abundant fruits and vegetables alongside homemade goods which created a vivid display of colors as they basked in the morning sunlight.

Gracie's peaceful expression in her last moments revealed an enduring beauty that remained present on her face. The passage of time had delicately carved lines into her skin which revealed her rich life experiences full of love. The vibrant hair Gracie once had had matured into soft strands that framed her face with an age-granted elegance.

The journey of life had tired her eyes but they retained their original depth and warmth that had enchanted me years before. The same remarkable eyes that sparkled with curiosity and mischief during our first encounter at the farmers market now display a beautiful serene glow. She peered through this world as if she had already witnessed the splendor waiting for her beyond.

The years had transformed her once smooth fair skin into a gentle softness resembling the petals of a cherished flower. Her high cheekbones lost their gentle blush which faded into a pale radiant glow indicating her lasting grace and power. Her lips which were naturally pink exhibited a tender softness that resonated with her gentle spirit.

Gracie's beauty extended beyond her physical appearance even during her last moments. Her beauty revealed her inner self through her kindness and her steadfast love and resilience toward her family.

The dimples that formed during her laughter had become faint but the memory of her laughter stayed strong in my mind as it resonated throughout our shared years.

Holding her hand brought back memories of how her hands had given comfort to me and our children along with love and support to everyone who knew her. These hands demonstrated resilience and elegance throughout life's challenges while they supported me during all our shared moments of happiness and grief.

The hard work Gracie performed on the family business combined with her active lifestyle had once created her slender yet strong build which time had made more fragile. Despite her weakened physical state she demonstrated an inner strength that revealed her remarkable character.

Over time her style maintained its simplicity and tastefulness while her natural elegance remained prominent. Gracie showed undeniable natural beauty and grace whether she wore a modest floral-patterned dress or practical work clothing.

As I watched her serene expression I recognized the girl who captured my heart many years earlier. The lively young woman had won my heart with her infectious laughter and kind spirit. Despite approaching the end of her journey, she still embodied the same beautiful strength that marked the amazing life we experienced together.

During those last precious seconds I understood that Gracie possessed a timeless beauty which went beyond the physical changes brought by aging. She possessed an inner beauty that emerged through years of love and laughter along with countless treasured memories. My final farewell brought me to the understanding that her memory would remain permanently within me as proof of love's lasting strength.

The unimaginable occurred within moments as blood began to seep out beneath her feet which she looked at intently. She had passed. I bent forward feeling the heavy burden of loss while the truth of her passing settled deep within me.

Gracie passed away in September when the leaves started transforming into golden and amber colors. The atmosphere exuded a melancholic essence as summer warmth transitioned into autumn crispness. The soft rustling of autumn leaves in the breeze mirrored the silent transition of a season as well as Gracie's peaceful departure from life shortly before her birthday on October 26th.

As I reflected on her passing, the words of Emily Dickinson's poem "The Last Night that She Lived" came to mind, capturing the poignant and delicate moments surrounding the death of my beloved:

The Last Night that She Lived
*Emily Dickinson*

The last Night that She lived
It was a Common Night
Except the Dying—this to Us
Made Nature different

We noticed smallest things—Things
overlooked before
By this great light upon our Minds
Italicized—as 'twere.

As We went out and in
Between Her final Room
And Rooms where Those to be alive
Tomorrow were, a Blame

That Others could exist
While She must finish
quite A Jealousy for Her
arose So nearly infinite—

We waited while She passed—
It was a narrow time—
Too jostled were Our Souls to speak
At length the notice came.

She mentioned, and forgot—
Then lightly as a Reed
Bent to the Water, struggled scarce—
Consented, and was dead—

And We—We placed the Hair—
And drew the Head erect—And
then an awful leisure was
Belief to regulate—

Our shared lifetime stretched across many years of love but ultimately reached its conclusion with a final farewell. Memories of our shared life overwhelmed me while I sat holding her hand. Our shared life consisted of joyful moments and difficult times but above all it was our love that helped us overcome everything.

I couldn't accept that my vibrant companion of seventy-five years had departed from this world.

I brought my mind back to the present moment and took one final look at Gracie's serene face. Throughout our journey we experienced love and laughter along with endless treasured times. Our story unfolded with wonder and joy at every stage from our initial encounter at the farmers market to our final farewell. In that moment of holding Gracie's hand I realized our love would persist beyond time and space. 1949 marks the year when my story began and remains eternally imprinted in my memory. On our first date beneath a starry sky I experienced some nervousness while initiating our first kiss. Our love began with that kiss which blossomed into an eternal bond able to withstand life's challenges while thriving under its joys. From that instant forward our lives became intertwined and we shared a profound and permanent love.

Our enduring love story expanded in depth with every single day as years transformed into decades. Together we constructed our life journey which was abundant with laughter and dreams alongside numerous shared experiences. The strength we discovered in each other allowed our bond to grow stronger while we moved through life's highs and lows. Our shared history grew richer as we celebrated birthdays and anniversaries along with the simple joys that filled our everyday lives.

Through the years we encountered many difficulties which tested our endurance however our love continued to stay strong. Our bond sustained us during sickness and grief while our unbreakable connection provided constant comfort. Our love persisted as a radiant light which served as hope and comfort in a constantly changing world even through the passage of many years.

Our last chapter together brought me back by her side where I cherished every single moment. Our hospital bed situated in the living room stood as a testament to our lasting love because it was where we spent our remaining days together. Amidst our suffering and uncertainty we discovered profound peace because our life together had been rich with love and devotion.

When she passed away her eyes sparkled with calm serenity which filled me with gratitude for our shared life. The loss she left was deeply profound yet demonstrated our love's powerful strength. I kissed her forehead gently and whispered my final farewell while understanding our love would persist eternally in my heart.

Even though she has left this world, our shared love will continue to exist within me indefinitely. This love exists beyond time and space and it has helped form my identity while continuing to direct me through future days. Our love story began with a kiss in 1949 and ended with a final kiss on her coffin. Between the first and final kiss existed a lifetime full of memories and moments alongside love that will remain unforgettable.

## Chapter Two

# Eggs and Emotions: A Love Story in the Marketplace

O ur family farm woke up to the sun sending its golden beams across the fields as another ordinary day began. My mother's chickens exceeded all expectation by producing far more eggs than we could ever eat. I took our excess eggs to sell at the Farmers' Market Association with baskets filled to the brim.

The small-town marketplace in 1949 buzzed with activity where fresh produce aromas blended with the friendly conversations between farmers and townspeople. The marketplace displayed aisles and stalls filled with fresh fruits and vegetables along with homemade items which created an animated scene as their bright colors shimmered in the morning sun.

I felt comfortable performing the egg-selling routine as it had become second nature to me. During that morning while I waited for John Herr to complete the egg counting and candling at the produce section, something unexpected happened. A young girl whom I believed I had never encountered stood close by. Her hair gleamed in the sunlight while her eyes appeared to contain endless curiosity. She prepared to be counted with her crates of eggs standing beside her. When our eyes locked I felt a silent yet intense spark come alive inside me. I swallowed with nervousness and finally found the courage to say hello timidly. Her smile was soft and knowing as it told me she felt the same thing. I didn't know who she was yet but our brief interaction launched a journey I never foresaw. When I spotted her again in the pickup with her father Martin Friske, that's when I learned her last name.

Our paths crossed again that evening during the Saturday night dance at KC's. Every Saturday night at the KC Hall our small town's social heartbeat was reflected in the dances. The upstairs hall came to life with youthful energy while the music bounced from one wall to another. Gracefully seated on the south side bench dancers wore brightly colored dresses which stood out beautifully in the gentle light. We boys assembled on the other side of the room where nervous excitement ran through us. The ritual was simple but thrilling: To dance with a girl, you approach her and ask her to join you for the dance. We aimed to participate in as many dances as we could with different girls because each dance represented a fresh experience.

I saw Gracie that evening. By then, I knew her name. She had a warm smile while her eyes revealed an infectious liveliness. She possessed an elegant charm which attracted me. I mustered all the bravery I could find and approached her on the dance floor to ask her to dance. She gave me a gentle nod to accept, and as we danced to the music I immediately felt connected to her. The melody briefly disappeared and during that time we seemed to be the only pair present in the room. Throughout the entire night we were together, we talked and laughed between dances until we found a comfortable harmony with each other.

Her father was downstairs playing dominos at his mother's house. Because he had brought her to town, I did not take her home. As I departed from the hall, I felt an inescapable sense that something special had started.

## *Chapter Three*

# Romance in the 1940s

T he atmosphere once contained the vibrant thrill of young people and the anticipation of weekend fun. My mastery of going on dates with minimal spending was a skill developed through necessity and creative thinking. Hopeful young men started their weekends at Joe Trachea's drug store, which served as their meeting place to plan evening outings. The old-fashioned crank phone located in the store's back room served as the town's social network connection point. The operator became our key to finding potential dates because of her extensive knowledge about everyone in town.

The stakes were particularly serious because my twin sisters had become the object of every young man's interest. People dreaded the embarrassment of asking one sister on a date only to discover she was already taken, which forced her twin sister to face an awkward situation. Keen suitors secretly questioned the operator to discover which twin was free to maximize their dating prospects. Anna Doris Geray was the girl who gave me my first date experience. She made the initiative to ask me out, which relieved me from the stress of approaching her first. Our group attended the Junior/Senior prom held at Schuzten-Hall located in downtown Lindsay. The night when I danced to "I Will Keep a Light in my Window Tonight" while surrounded by twinkling lights stands as the memorable start of my dating life.

I frequently went on double-dates with my friends Ruben Sturm, William Joseph Miller, Herbie Miller, and James Bayer. Ruben's '38 four-door Chevrolet sedan with deteriorated knee action front wheels was my first double date ride with worn-out wheels. Our evenings out became exciting because the car's dangerous state added an extra element of risk. My dad supported me by lending his gas-filled car and giving me a dollar to spend that night. We paid twenty-five cents to enter the movie and spent the remaining money on soda and hamburgers at the nearby diner.

The excitement of triple-dating reached new heights when Bill Miller and Ruben Sturm joined in. Bill Miller fell for Teresa Walter while Ruben Sturm developed a serious relationship with Bernice Lutmer. My dating choices revolved around going out with whoever seemed available. Our expeditions became epic adventures during the rainy season especially when we had to bring Bernice back to her road that was prone to flooding. Helen Waltersheid, Teresa Rohmer, Gracie Wimmer, Imogene Bezner, Betty Jean Fleitman, Rose Becker and Barbara Miller made up my dating list. Each girl brought unique challenges and experiences. The adventure involved driving on muddy roads to reach Helen's house and opening several gates for Barbara before escorting Teresa home during rainstorms while getting soaked. Our shared memories include annual trips to the Dallas state fair alongside movie nights at the local theater during which we indulged in youthful fun. Barbara Miller informed me during one drive home that she was moving away which marked our final date together. I gave Barbara my best wishes for her upcoming journey.

I always had a strange feeling with each girl I dated. It was lingering feeling that something was lacking.

*Chapter Four*

# Love Blossoms

T he post-war era brought new beginnings. I began my job at the phone company while proudly displaying my new two-door green Plymouth Sedan as I drove around town. People saw it as an emblem of fresh opportunities and independence. The accident resulted in a broken leg which required me to rest at home during my recovery period. That period brought on my longing for more meaningful experiences and deeper fulfillment.

Our initial meeting at the farmers market brought Gracie back to my memory. She remained a high school junior when she first met me yet she made a memorable impact on me. I made the decision to invite her to go on a date.

James Bayer and I shared double dates with our friends where we enjoyed youthful excitement while traveling on the open road. One afternoon James expressed his interest in going out with "that Friske girl". Sensing that quick action was necessary, I decided to ask Gracie out before James could. I continued with my plans despite being on crutches because of an injury. I contacted Gracie to ask her to go out with me next Saturday. To my delight, she agreed. James sighed and confessed that he wanted to ask her out before I did.

The first time we went out together happened in 1949, and it met all my expectations. An extraordinary connection appeared between us from our first meeting, which I never before experienced with anyone else. Our discussions moved smoothly and her laughter sounded like a beautiful melody. I sensed she felt the same connection. Gracie possessed that unique ability to make me comfortable while during our dances she appeared to dissolve into my embrace. We moved as one entity while experiencing both excitement and surprise about our deep connection.

I waited several days before asking her out again because I was eager to see her once more. To my disappointment, she already had plans. She offered me advice with a warm smile, "I suggest you call earlier next time." I made a call to another girl on her line hoping to catch Gracie's attention while knowing her mother could be listening. Gracie discovered I had called another girl on her party line which sparked jealousy that led her to accept all my subsequent invitations.

Although she was only a 15-year-old girl, her composure and mature demeanor revealed a wisdom not expected from someone her age. We started dating steadily then because our relationship grew stronger every day.

The presence of curious listeners on the party line always remained in my mind during our phone calls. My position as the telephone man gave me benefits because I installed a hidden button on the switchboard for operators to use whenever I wanted to reach Gracie. The new phone button enabled me to call her privately which preserved some privacy for our new relationship.

Gracie and I experienced thrilling moments of discovery during our initial days together. Her impact on me was unlike any girl I had ever encountered before. We talked for endless hours together while laughter filled the air and her presence introduced me to new happiness. We seemed to be two parts of a single entity united by an unseen power.

Gracie's beauty was remarkable, but her kindness and intelligence were even more impressive. Her view of the world captivated me and her words held my complete attention. We shared deep conversations about our families as well as our dreams for the future and every discussion strengthened our bond.

Despite our age difference, there was an undeniable bond forming between us, one that was built on mutual respect and admiration. The spark that had ignited the day we first met grew into a flame, warming our hearts and lighting up our lives.

Our age gap couldn't stop the formation of a strong connection between us because we built our friendship on shared respect and admiration. The initial spark from our first meeting expanded into a flame that warmed our hearts and illuminated our lives.

We would never have predicted how much our accidental encounter would direct our life paths. The quiet initial attraction we felt couldn't have possibly developed into a love that lasted close to seventy-five years. The marketplace and KC's dance floor became the backdrop where we lost ourselves in conversation and laughter that formed the first pages of our love story.

And so, under the observant eyes of the townsfolk and with the morning sun shining gently above us, Gracie and I started our journey together which would stand as a testament to love, resilience and shared memories throughout our lifetime. The marketplace provided us with more than just a venue for selling eggs; it gave us the start of our beautiful love story.

*Chapter Five*

# Duty and Departure: Leaving My Love Behind

My relationship with Gracie became serious during the warm months of late spring between May and June in 1949. Gracie's presence gave me an overwhelming sense of invincibility while I marveled at the promising world around me. But fate had other plans. My military service began when I was drafted by the U.S. in December 1950. Armed Forces. Gracie at sixteen was making her way through her final year in high school. We couldn't marry because she was too young and I didn't want to hold her youthful spirit back while I faced a distant and uncertain future.

The moment I got ready to depart I experienced a deep weight press down upon my heart. What sort of request could I possibly make to have her suspend her life while I served abroad? Whenever I imagined her sharing laughter with another person my heart twisted painfully. Gracie went through the mixed emotions of teenage milestones by herself including the junior/senior prom and graduation happiness as well as the shared whispers and giggles that we should have experienced together. She refused to go to any other boy because she was loyal to me. Her invitation for my younger brother Jerry to be her prom escort deeply moved me.

My six-month stay at Fort Hood, Texas was dedicated to basic training. The weekdays were filled with exhausting drills and strict discipline yet weekends provided a strong sense of hope. I never missed a weekend when I drove the 300-mile trip home to visit Gracie. The new car transformed into a vessel of determination as it tracked miles like love letters inscribed on asphalt. My Gainesville friends Ewald Fuhrmann, Joe Phillips, and Hugh Perry frequently accompanied me on the lengthy drives and their shared laughter provided a pleasant diversion. During that time our routes consisted of an assortment of side roads which necessitated us to navigate past every hamlet situated between Killeen and my residence. The distance diminished between us with each mile I traveled because nothing else held significance. The move marked a turning point for us as it created new physical and emotional distance between us. Following my basic training I received orders which required me to travel across the ocean to Germany. I brought my car home to leave it with family members on the day I was deployed. Bill and Gracie took me to Dallas where I boarded the train headed for Fort Hood to begin my deployment. The goodbye was wrenching. Gracie pressed close as I held her while her hair's fragrance etched itself into my mind; I murmured "I'll be back before you know it," even though I knew we wouldn't see each other for 18 months.

During my final pickup from her new home before departing for deployment I witnessed an unsettling scene. As I walked up to the house I noticed Harold Nortman standing there. He was convinced I was already gone and saw this as his chance to win Gracie's affection. Upon recognizing my presence he pretended to be astonished and explained he had come to visit Joan who is Gracie's younger sister. Unease twisted into a knot within my stomach.

Gracie's parents held a distrust toward me for reasons that remained unclear to me. They appeared determined to remove her from my company because I might soon leave or because of parental protective instincts. They advised her to maintain friendships and seek emotional support from someone available like Harold. Gracie found herself trapped between societal demands and personal emotional struggles.

After graduation, Gracie sought independence. Gracie found employment at the Kress five-and-dime store in Gainesville and relocated to live with her grandmother on North Weaver Street. The move served as a bold statement of her self-determination.

*Chapter Six*

# Letters Across the Sea

During my time in service Gracie and I maintained our romantic connection by regularly sending letters to each other. Weekly letters allowed us to express our deepest emotions through written words. My entire two-year service depended on our correspondence because it kept us connected. Every envelope transported delicate expressions of love alongside narratives from the days that separated us.

However, challenges persisted. Gracie received her letters through her parents' farm but her mother took actions which worsened their already tense relationship. Her mother claimed that I had ceased writing to her, which planted seeds of doubt. But Gracie's intuition told her otherwise. She kept up her resourceful ways by establishing contact with the postal workers in Gainesville. The postal workers felt sympathetic toward her situation, so they quietly delivered the letters using an alternate path instead of the standard procedure. The written correspondence crossed the divide between us through expressions of love and yearning.

Eventually the letters started coming less frequently. Our parents manipulated our paths to lead us apart before my anticipated return. Gracie's grandmother pushed for a local boy whom she believed was an honorable match for her granddaughter. My intuition proved right when I discovered it was Harold. Unbeknownst to me, Harold had ulterior motives. He planned to wed Gracie before my return while exploiting her vulnerable situation. Her parents intensified this stress by pressuring Gracie to choose him and break off her relationship with me. The unyielding pressure compelled Gracie to write a deeply emotional Dear John letter which struck its recipient with unexpected force. Her letter stated that during my absence she began seeing a local farmer and they started a romantic relationship. During my absence she found support and companionship through her new relationship. She remained undecided about completely severing ties and seemed to want to observe whether time and distance would change our relationship.

December 1952 finally arrived. My heart raced when our ship made port in New York City. An army aircraft with two engines took us directly to Fort Hood where we received our discharge. As soon as I set foot in Texas I knew exactly where I needed to be. Directly after my arrival in Gainesville I headed to the Sears Store since that's where Gracie worked. Finding Gracie in the store aisles felt like seeing an illusion transform into reality. I immediately closed the gap between us to hold her and planted a kiss on her lips. She remained close to me without resistance, but her response suggested hesitancy which created an unexpected separation between us.

Within me existed an internal struggle where confusion clashed with hope. Gracie kept meeting Harold and his lingering presence served as a continuous reminder of the barriers we needed to overcome. A twist of fate led us to Johnny Schmitz's club on the opposite side of the river one evening. I sat alone with a drink and my racing thoughts until Gracie came up to me. Her eyes showed both determination and vulnerability.

"I'm finished with Harold," she announced quietly before asking if I would escort her home. Relief and joy flooded my senses. Harold became aggressive over time and his advances remained uncontrolled while he pursued selfish goals. Out of desperation he broke limits and showed Gracie a side of him she could not tolerate. She understood that despite the obstacles between us our bond remained sincere and respectful.

The moment we exited the club together marked the start of my renewed sense of purpose. I confronted the unknown future with confidence because Gracie stood with me. The progression of our journey faced numerous challenges from time constraints to external stress yet we continuously reunited. Beneath the starlit sky I understood that our shared story had just reopened its pages.

## Chapter Seven

# Roots of Resilience: Gracie's Family History

A journey through her family history reveals the depth of Gracie's spirit and the kindness evident in each of her actions. Gracie's character developed through perseverance, integrity, and unwavering love which she inherited from many generations of the Friske family. The values and strength her family taught her became evident in her character through every experience and lesson she learned. By examining Gracie's family history we discover the core values that formed her worldview. The journey uncovers how historical echoes shape today's world and create a woman whose strength and compassion influence countless lives.

The exploration of Gracie's ancestral background helps us understand the foundational strength that kept her grounded. Her story represents the ongoing legacy that previous generations established through their enduring love and unyielding integrity combined with everyday heroism when faced with extraordinary challenges. Martin and Martha Friske entered the world during the beginning of the 20th century where they encountered both opportunities and difficulties. Martin was born on December 19,

1901 and Martha arrived in this world just months earlier on August 15, 1901. Martin playfully noted their shared birth year which demonstrated the strong connection between him and Martha. Gracie developed her character from the resilient partnership of Martin and Martha who supported each other through life's toughest challenges.

The story of the Friske family took place during the Great Depression, a tough time when many families faced serious economic challenges. This hardship affected their choices and futures in deep ways. For Martin and Martha, these struggles were very real and significant.

Joe Luke, Martin and Martha's brother, dedicated himself to managing the Muenster Mill. The mill stood for their aspirations and ambitions beyond being a simple business venture. Troubles emerged when Martin started to suspect that there were financial issues. The mill they worked hard to develop ended up being sold to Joe Felderhoff because of their economic struggles and doubts. Their family faced both financial losses and intense emotional challenges which tested their bonds and strengthened their resilience.

Martin and Martha relocated to Hereford, Texas to begin anew and committed themselves to farming as their way of life. The endless stretches of land and clear skies presented endless possibilities for what they could create. The birth of their two daughters Myrtle and Toni Mae brought joy and laughter to their modest home during their time in Hereford. Yet, the land proved unforgiving. A seven-year drought transformed fertile soil into dust and dried up hopes along with the withered crops. The persistent sun stripped the earth of life while simultaneously burdening their emotional resilience and financial resources.

The Friskes decided to go back to Muenster despite the tough choice they faced. With heavy debt hanging over them they departed Hereford while holding firmly onto their moral principles. They worked tirelessly for twelve years until they finally returned to Hereford to pay off their debts demonstrating their unwavering integrity. When the Friskes could not locate their creditors they sent their repayments to the church to maintain their ethical balance.

Gracie's childhood was filled with tales about perseverance and strong ethical standards. The Great Depression era taught Gracie's parents not only about surviving tough times but also demonstrated their enduring determination and moral bravery. Her parents taught her that adversity requires dignity and that challenges allow a person to develop their character.

Gracie always pictured Grandma Friske as a small woman who demonstrated perfect punctuality and proper behavior throughout her entire life. Her fine physique combined with perfectly arranged clothing allowed her to navigate the world while maintaining a composed sense of dignity. A distant aloofness hid behind the polished surface which made family events feel overshadowed. The older woman stayed aloof and unresponsive to her children's attempts to create a warm bond because she showed her affection only toward Arnold's children. Martin Friske started managing the family farm after August Friske chose to retire. The property extended over 300 acres and lay three miles west of Muenster. The region remained untouched by any asphalt paths because Highway 82 was not yet built allowing agricultural land to extend without interruption toward the distant horizon.

As per tradition during that era Gracie entered the world in her family's home back in 1933. She had multiple siblings and her younger sisters Joan and Jere were born later. The Friske household buzzed with children's laughter while parents frequently played ball with them outdoors to create a loving and supportive family atmosphere.

The construction of Highway 82 in 1936 changed Gracie's world when she was only a few years old. A newly built road ran across their property which split the farm into two distinct properties. The northern part continued to be managed by Martin while Arnold Friske and his wife Delores took up residence on the southern farm during their initial years together before relocating to Gainesville.

The northern farm contained an old two-story house that stood next to multiple outbuildings. Gracie had clear memories of sitting on an extended bench at the dinner table while the family ate Martha's home-cooked meals. The children found adventure and mischief on the creaky stairs that led to the second floor. At approximately five or six years old Gracie witnessed her parents demolish the old house to make way for a new single-story home. Their two-bedroom home provided limited space for their family of four girls and one boy yet they managed to live successfully in it. Throughout construction time the whole family resided in the garage which led to a lasting memory filled with togetherness and adaptability.

The summer, when Gracie turned six years old, she looked after her little sister Jere while their mother worked in the fields. The shared responsibilities and joint effort shown through their work exemplified the nature of farm life. Electricity did not exist on the Friske farm which deprived them of several modern amenities. To maintain battery power for their radio listening they used a wind charger which provided them vital access to the outside world. During the evenings the family used kerosene lamps for lighting which provided a warm glow as the children assembled at the kitchen table to finish their homework.

Storing food properly became an ongoing problem when there was no refrigerator available. Martin bought a block of ice every Sunday morning after church to place into their icebox which helped them cope briefly with the Texas temperatures. Their perishables stayed cool inside the icebox until the ice finally melted.

Without a refrigerator, food preservation was a constant challenge. Every Sunday morning after church, Martin would purchase a block of ice to place in their icebox, providing temporary relief from the Texas heat. The icebox was a simple luxury that kept their perishables cool until the ice inevitably melted away.

The farm served as both a workplace and a vast playground that overflowed with adventure. The chicken house had a slanted roof and stood next to the area where the cattle grazed. The siblings found joy in ascending to the roof and then jumping down to the cow lot's soft ground. The kids always emerged laughing from the cow lot splattered with mud and cow droppings despite their mother's feigned disapproval. The fresh earthy scent became connected to joyful sibling play during afternoon leisure time.

The area north of the farmhouse featured a timbered landscape with a running creek that served as the setting for numerous journeys of exploration. Rainfall brought about new adventures for the children as they explored the woods climbing trees and designing games born from youthful imagination. The creek acted as the dividing line between their property and the neighboring land although natural forces frequently challenged this separation. Heavy rains would wash away their makeshift water gap, which required family labor to rebuild so their cattle wouldn't stray—a necessary task that became part of their rural life.

The farm life presented a colorful blend of laborious effort, enduring strength, and daily simple pleasures. Gracie's early years unfolded through the cycles of seasons and the necessities of farm work. Despite the constant hard work they faced, there was plenty of love and laughter throughout their lives. They developed both determination and strong family connections through their repeated efforts to fix the water gap and their adaptation to living without modern conveniences.

Gracie developed a deep understanding of perseverance and found beauty in everyday moments during her formative years. Her youthful experiences molded her into a woman who stands firm in her faith and draws strength from family love while remaining steadfast through life's unavoidable challenges.

Gracie remembered the winding county road that ran through the central countryside linking her grandfather's two farms. The cows followed this road every day for grazing in a manner that seemed as instinctive as breathing. The eastern boundary of the north farm marked the property of Dangelmayr which featured a stunning grove of trees that provided shade and served as an ideal play area for Gracie and her sisters. The girls climbed into the tree branches as they watched their cows eat contentedly and experienced their adventurous bliss.

Amidst a group of sisters, Gracie took on the role of her father' s willing assistant with enthusiasm. She became familiar with all aspects of farm life by becoming proficient in tractor operation and field plowing while also learning how to harrow and work through the demanding tasks of picking cotton and corn. Her father and she processed shocked grain while remaining vigilant of the hidden dangers present in the tall grass where snakes waited. Gracie tested her physical abilities while helping her father stack loose hay in the barn since they did not have machines and depended on pitchforks and physical labor.

The farm was fraught with challenges, particularly from thieves. They kept gas in 55-gallon barrels, yet it always seemed to vanish mysteriously. Their chickens, too, were never safe; just as they reached fryer size, someone would snatch them away. One fateful morning, Gracie's mother discovered a man's handkerchief in the chicken house. Suspecting foul play, she speculated that the handkerchief had been used to quiet the chickens with chloroform. Undeterred, she placed an ad in the Muenster Newspaper, asking the owner to come and reclaim it, but the handkerchief remained unclaimed, just like their missing chickens.

One night before they had yard lights, Gracie's mother felt a surge of determination when she thought she saw a figure near the barn. A skilled shot, she retrieved her .410 shotgun, loading it with a mix of bravado and anxiety. When she fired, the silhouette dropped to the ground, sending a chill through her heart—what if she had harmed a person? Restless and guilt-ridden, she hardly slept that night.

The dawn brought clarity as she approached the scene of her midnight panic, only to find a very dead owl lay there, shot cleanly between its eyes. Over time, the neighborhood changed, and eventually, one certain neighbor moved away, yielding them the freedom to keep their fryers for themselves without fear of loss.

Gracie chuckled as she remembered the property they called home, often boasting that it had the most edge rocks in the entire county. Jokingly, they informed August Friske, Martin's father, that he had purchased the rockiest land available. On the farm, Gracie and her sister Myrtle took pride in their diligent work, while Toni and Joan often found ways to avoid it. Toni, in particular, was notorious for claiming she had a backache whenever chores loomed.

Life changed when they moved to the farm south of the highway when Gracie was twelve. With her father expanding his farming endeavors to both properties, the family soon experienced a bit of modernity; electricity finally graced their home on the south farm, filling their lives with the marvels of a refrigerator, electric lights, and even a radio. Yet, some remnants of the past lingered—no water heater yet, and they still relied on an outhouse.

One Sunday while their parents were away, Toni's boyfriend, Ray Lueb, visited. Kind-hearted, he offered to help the kids with milking, a task that sometimes proved challenging. Getting a good laugh, Gracie and Myrtle watched as Ray attempted to handle the particularly stubborn cow they had given him. The sight of him struggling made the work lighter, mixed with laughter that echoed through the barn—a moment that filled their simple farm life with joy and camaraderie.

Gracie often thought about her oldest sister, Myrtle, who had a way of attracting attention. Myrtle dated many different boys, but their parents never approved of any of them. In fact, their mother had once gone so far as to buy a birthday card and send it to one of Myrtle's crushes, pretending it was from her. Gracie chuckled at the memory; Myrtle eventually caught on to their mother's schemes.

When Myrtle left home to attend nurse's school in Galveston, Gracie felt a mixture of pride and loss. Myrtle returned after finishing her training and began working at M & S Hospital. It was during World War II that she met her first husband. He was stationed at Camp Howze and would come to visit, staying overnight at their house. The next day, their parents took them to see the priest, and they got married right away. Back then, girls didn't spend the night at their boyfriends' houses, and Gracie remembered feeling uneasy about this man. He had a rough way of speaking, often using "Jesus Christ" as a casual curse, which bothered her. Gracie was just twelve or thirteen then, and one day, she mustered the courage to ask him why he talked like that. To her surprise, she never heard him say it again.

As she looked back, Gracie sometimes blamed their parents for what had happened. Mom and Dad had someone local picked out for Myrtle, too, and Gracie was sure that would have turned out badly. Their parents often tried to choose their future husbands, including Alvin, who was another boy they disapproved of. Gracie didn't have many memories of living with Myrtle, as she was nine years older and had left home when Gracie was still young.

Myrtle and Toni both attended grade school at Sacred Heart because there was no high school in Muenster at the time. Myrtle continued her education at Saint Mary's in Gainesville, where she made quite the entrance, riding to school on the back of Bill Luke's motorcycle. Meanwhile, Toni went her own way, heading off to high school in Wichita Falls. In those years, each sister carved out her own path, but Gracie often felt the pull of their shared memories and the love that wove them together as family.

Gracie attended Sacred Heart High School during a time of change when the school was trying to merge with the Muenster Public School. It was a challenging period; the public school claimed Sacred Heart's football mascot and colors, even taking the water heater from the locker room. This transition marked the birth of the Tigers, and it created a split in Gracie's class. About half of her classmates chose to switch to the public school. They had started together in first grade, with thirty students, but only twelve graduated from Sacred Heart School alongside her. Despite the rising tuition, Gracie stuck with her school, loyal to the community and the friendships she had formed.

Sports were a huge part of Gracie's life. She loved playing volleyball and basketball at school. In the summers, she joined a baseball team that competed against teams from the Gainesville Training School and the Southwestern Bell Telephone operators. Each day, she would walk three miles into town for practice and then walk three miles back home afterward. It was a different era, and Gracie often smiled when thinking about how you rarely saw kids do that now. In softball, she played as the hind catcher, while in basketball, she was positioned as guard during the games when the girls played half court. Her role meant she rarely had to shoot the ball, but the competition was fierce, especially against the girls from the training school—who were known for being tough.

In the evenings, if Gracie needed to go somewhere in town, her dad would take her. After dropping her off, he'd head over to Grandma and Grandpa Friske's house until she was done. Sometimes, Gracie would join in the game of dominoes, where Grandpa would always want her as his partner. Those moments were filled with laughter, strategizing over the dominoes, and the warmth of family connection. Even through the ups and downs of school life and sports, Gracie treasured these simple times spent with her family, finding joy in the little things that made every day special.

Family roots of the Friskes demonstrate principles of perseverance and integrity that have been handed down through multiple generations. Martin and Martha guided their family through the Great Depression's trials by maintaining their deep love and steadfast partnership. The Friske family demonstrated resilience when they moved from the Muenster Mill to Hereford farming and chose to return to Muenster to maintain their moral standards despite facing adversity.

Her childhood memories which included laughter and sibling camaraderie remained vivid as they faced rural life challenges together. The difficulties associated with traditional farming methods combined with the happiness derived from basic life's enjoyments.

Gracie reflected deeply on her family's enduring hardships which taught her lasting lessons about resilience and love while uncovering beauty in everyday experiences. The events of her life created her identity foundation while developing into a compassionate and strong woman who accepted all life's trials. Her family's narrative served as her guiding light from within her heart while she moved forward into her then uncertain future.

## *Chapter Eight*

# Journey into Love:
# Our Marriage

When I came back from Army service I entered a world that was familiar yet completely altered. The small town streets appeared more confined while faces displayed both nostalgic memories and gentle detachment. I resumed my job at the telephone company where I found myself responsible for the operation while it served as my sanctuary. Bill departed from his post to travel to Saint Louis, Missouri where he began his educational journey. During Herman Younger's absence Cotton Jackson managed the company as his brother-in-law. Upon my return to work Cotton Jackson immediately transferred complete operational control to me. I felt the heavy responsibility of ensuring the telephone company's operations but accepted this task with complete dedication.

The connection between Gracie and me reignited with a warmth that resembled embers coming back to life. Yet, new obstacles emerged. The firm opposition from her parents against our union created a lasting shadow that dimmed our happiness. Their prohibition against me picking her up at their house struck me with unexpected pain. To prevent this obstacle from affecting us I collaborated with my old friend James Bayer to create a strategy. We started to double date together which reminded us of our past experiences. James would first visit Gracie's house to pick her up and then collect his date for their double date. Our evenings together became special occasions where we shared laughter and stolen glances in dimly lit diners and danced side by side under starry skies at local venues. James would faithfully take Gracie back to her front door at night's end. Although the arrangement wasn't perfect we accepted this compromise so we could spend time together.

Gracie became tired of living with deception as months went by. During a fresh autumn afternoon while leaves danced around our feet she shared her secret with me. She chose to rent Marie Geray's room in order to establish her own independence and begin anew outside her parents' household. Her courageous choice increased my respect for her powerful spirit.

With this newfound freedom, our relationship blossomed. The obstacles which separated us started to fall apart. I grasped Gracie's hands during an evening when the sun slipped under the horizon while the sky transformed into shades of amber and crimson. Her skin's soft texture sent tremors through my entire body as I murmured "Marry me" barely louder than the whispering trees. Time stopped moving when her eyes locked with mine in a searching gaze. Her face lit up with a radiant smile. "Yes," she replied, the word filling me with a joy I hadn't known possible.

I understood that trying to get her father's approval would be pointless. His steadfast disapproval persisted and I wanted to protect our joy from any obstacles. Our future became the focal point of our silent planning sessions. My purchase of three lots on 624 North Cedar Street gave me purpose because I envisioned building our first home on this land. The plots I bought were $600 each while I took out a $6,500 loan from Frank Trubenbach to build the house. Fresh timber aroma and hammer sounds surrounded me as I employed Tony and Eugene Klement to make our vision a reality. As each wall grew higher through the rhythmic hammering of nails we envisioned our future together. Henry Henscheid used his legendary painting skills to transform the rooms into spaces full of warmth and personality. We prioritized completing enough of the house for our move-in after the wedding while planning to finish rooms together as a newlywed couple.

On October 20, 1953 our wedding day greeted us with a crisp morning atmosphere filled with the world's shimmering anticipation. Father Conrad was to lead the ceremony starting at 9 a.m. at Lindsay church. People wondered if Gracie's father would attend her wedding and if he would walk her down the aisle. Should he fail to appear, I planned to join Gracie at the rear of the church before proceeding together toward our shared future. The organ started playing when the weighty oak doors opened to reveal him standing beside his daughter holding her hand with a serious look.

My feelings of overwhelming emotion caused me to misjudge the width of the doorway as I exited the sacristy to meet my bride which resulted in me hitting my head against the vigil light. An intense pain pulsed through me but the moment Gracie came into view with her veil softly hiding her glowing face everything else became irrelevant. I started to feel the dull pain at the spot where my head hit only when I was surrounded by laughter and the sound of glasses clinking during the reception.

The ceremony brought together a close group of people who deeply cared about us. Randy Bayer took the role of my best man because his brother James was serving in the military and couldn't attend. Joan Geray was Gracie's cherished friend who served as bridesmaid. The joy of our wedding day comes through in the smiles of our wedding photographs.

We held our reception at 6 p.m. in the old parish hall's cozy basement. Time slipped away quickly during those hours as we experienced pure bliss. The town's celebrated chef Agnes Lehnertz created a mouthwatering feast which filled the hall with enticing scents of roasted meats and freshly baked bread. Both of us cherished countless memories from the old VFW hall on South Main Street where we held our wedding dance. After the dance floor's expansion we became the first couple to glide across its polished surface. When the band began "The Waltz You Saved for Me," Gracie and I moved together as one person while the world melted away into a dreamlike scene of smiling faces and gentle lights.

We took precautions knowing our well-meaning friends planned playful pranks. We concealed our vehicle in Gainesville by storing it inside the garage of Gracie's Sears boss named Marguerite. Wilde Chevrolet provided us with a car for our wedding, which enabled us to escape unnoticed. Robert Bayer assisted us in retrieving our hidden car after the celebration ended. We started our marital journey beneath a starry sky while facing an uncertain future ahead.

## Chapter Nine

# A Journey of Firsts: Our Honeymoon Memories

T hroughout our honeymoon we experienced a series of small adventures that led to shared discoveries. Our first night on our honeymoon took place at an adorable motel located in Ardmore, Oklahoma. This room had simple features yet appeared to us like a luxurious hotel suite. As we traveled to Vinita, Oklahoma the following day we witnessed gentle waves of rolling hills stretching beneath open skies. After traveling for three days we arrived at Saint Louis to spend time with my brother Bill who was deeply engaged in his education at Loyola University. We enjoyed a meal with the Theisens who were close friends to Grandmother Fuhrman at their residence. Their hospitality warmed us but journey fatigue overpowered us so we ended up sleeping at the dinner table which amused everyone.

We traveled from Saint Louis to Lincoln, Nebraska so that I could visit my brother Jerry at Marquette University. As we reunited, cherished memories surfaced when we introduced Gracie as the newest member of our family. Our route led us across South Dakota's broad plains heading west. Our honeymoon featured a memorable night spent in Oglala where the stars appeared so close to the ground that the silence became incredibly intense.

Through our travels we reached the stunning vistas of Colorado Springs. The atmosphere possessed a crystalline quality which transported pine aromas together with winter's imminent arrival. While exploring the Garden of the Gods we stood in awe of its massive red rock structures that appeared to belong to another world. We set out to drive up Pikes Peak seeking adventure but encountered unexpected challenges from the weather conditions in late October. A closed gate stopped us since ice covered the route making it too dangerous to proceed. We continued our exploration of the historic mining town of Cripple Creek where remnants of the Gold Rush era lingered in its old wooden buildings and narrow streets.

The arrival of dusk guided us onto a 32-mile serpentine mountain path leading to Canon City, Colorado. The underdeveloped road twisted through the rugged terrain and was only slightly wider than our car. Some sections of the road were one-way while narrow passing areas were built along stretches for vehicles to overtake each other. The darkness became our shroud transforming the drive into a trial of courage and mutual confidence. We did not know at that moment that the car's generator had stopped working. The vehicle operated purely on battery power during our ride which became apparent to us only the following day. It felt as though some guardian angel appeared to guard us throughout that night.

The photos we took during our trip consisted mostly of motel signs and indistinct landscapes because our excitement during the journey took precedence over taking pictures. Despite their lack of artistic quality these pictures served as precious records of the happy spontaneity we shared in our early weeks together.

After moving to our Cedar Street home we worked on final details to transform the house into a personal sanctuary. Gracie resumed her job at the Sears mail-order location situated on California Street in Gainesville. She spent her days surrounded by customers and coworker friendships while I devoted my time to telephone company duties.

Life, however, presented us with trials. Gracie lost her pregnancies three times and we experienced these silent sorrows together in private. Uncertain dreams weighed us down as we questioned whether we would ever experience parenthood. Seven years after our wedding ceremony we decided to adopt a child in 1960. The addition of Kent to our family brought us immense happiness. When I first held him I experienced an immense wave of love and protective instincts.

As time passed by three more years life threw another unexpected surprise our way. During a Las Vegas vacation which represented a city of endless opportunities Gracie found herself pregnant. The year 1963 marked the birth of Gene who symbolized hope and resilience. Our family became whole which formed from our faith and enduring love together with our persistence.

During this period of personal achievements our awaited reconciliation came to pass. Gracie's mother asked to meet me shortly before she died. Time and introspection had transformed her once unyielding gaze into a softer expression. Her voice heavy with regret, she apologized for rejecting my role as her son-in-law before asking if I could forgive her while searching my eyes. I reassured her by telling her she didn't need to apologize for anything. Even from the very start, I had never harbored any negative feelings toward her or her husband.

Looking back on our journey through hardships and joyous moments fills my heart with deep appreciation. Together we constructed our shared existence which blossomed through everlasting love and mutual aspirations. Her laughter in our home halls and the pine smell on mountain roads alongside her hand touching mine stand out as vivid treasures from our shared journey. We journeyed through life with love and resilience which stands as proof of our steadfast dedication and the wonder that exists in every moment of happiness and difficulty.

## Chapter Ten

# Navigating Heartbreak: The Journey to Parenthood

While the path to becoming parents usually shows happiness and aspirations in pictures, our experience with Gracie felt like entering a turbulent storm filled with heartbreak and uncertainty. Our cherished hopeful moments merged with profound sadness that perpetually lingered over our lives like a shadow. Our dreams started with excitement about someday cradling our own baby while teaching them to walk and listening to their laughter fill our home. The harsh truth transformed our dreams into a series of devastating losses while pushing us to the limits of our perseverance.

The beginning of our marriage was marked by the devastating heartbreak of losing three pregnancies through miscarriage. Every heartbreaking experience felt like hope had been snuffed out before it could become the warmth of family life. The anxious anticipation remained in my memory as we waited for the doctor's news but were met instead with devastating silence. Gracie bore her sorrow in silence but I could read her anguish clearly in her face even as she pretended to smile at me. The shared sorrow we experienced served as a painful reminder of life's vulnerability while our cherished dreams appeared to vanish further with every heartbreak we suffered.

During our darkest moments we found hope through adoption and approached Catholic Charities in Dallas to start a new chapter by adopting a child. Kent joined our family two weeks after his birth in November 1960 which marked a fresh start after our period of sadness. We arrived at Saint Paul's Hospital in Dallas with our 1949 Plymouth two-door car which had been our choice vehicle for our honeymoon seven years prior.

The first time we held him erased the pain of our past with overwhelming joy. During our trip home I felt excitement rising up inside me. We made a stop at my parents' farm east of Muenster to present my mother with her first grandchild. A pregnant telephone operator nearby brought me a mixture of pride and awareness of our constant battles with life's rapid pace. The energetic young Kent brought laughter into our home in no time. He needed to be surrounded by people all the time. I joined him in playing games like ball-throwing or spontaneous playground activities every chance I got because I wanted to develop his innate abilities.

As time went by and Kent matured we discovered ourselves once again on an intricate journey. The joyful demeanor Kent once had vanished into unforeseen difficulties that dragged us back into serious concerns and hardships. His extroverted personality changed into restlessness which led him onto a troublesome journey. The day he stole a watch stands out in my memory because he wanted to impress Rummy Hess through that misguided act. He took pleasure in climbing yet the levels he reached posed serious dangers. My mind holds the image of him suspended upside down in the peach tree calling for assistance as his foot remained trapped between the branches while innocence battled against ambition.

Gene rode together with me to school every day but Kent chose to cycle there instead. Before sunrise each morning they performed their duties as altar boys.

As Kent grew, so did his struggles. His prominent overbite persisted because he removed his braces as soon as he left the dentist's office showing he wasn't prepared for that challenge. Kent's childhood nervousness led to constant sweating palms which created ongoing cycles of embarrassment and neglect. Even after many attempts to teach him about self-care he refused to listen and our home became increasingly shadowed by his stubborn refusal to change.

School was another battlefield. The impact of dyslexia turned his education into an obstacle filled path while I arranged for Sister Alberta to offer him additional support beyond regular school hours. Kent regularly avoided those extra lessons which demolished any chances of academic improvement. He departed Sacred Heart High School without earning a diploma and received only a blank slip symbolizing all his lost chances.

Upon his graduation Kent relocated to a trailer situated on the south side of Muenster. I made significant efforts to support him which included purchasing a big-screen TV for his home. When I visited his trailer the TV had disappeared because he pawning it for drugs. His future prospects kept spiraling back towards despair despite my hopes for him. He worked at our company but preferred to stay in the truck dreaming about his future authority. I arranged for Kent to work with Gene Gieb who had experience in the oil fields in order to teach him responsibility. His absence from work was brief because he quit without prior notice and persistently discovered ways to dodge his job responsibilities.

A significant change occurred when I arranged a trip to Germany and promised him a car as a reward if he stayed behind.

Kent decided to stay with my sister Elsie but he destroyed the Pontiac I had given him when I returned. The limited damage from his reckless driving was overshadowed by my frustration over his failure to manage basic responsibilities such as filling the gas tank. Upon discovering that fertilizer was dumped inside the car I was faced with the painful evidence of unpaid debts and neglected relationships.

In search of new beginnings I discovered a Fort Worth boys' home which promised hope for troubled youth. The Houston facility became Kent's new placement after I enrolled him in the Fort Worth program which promised a structured environment. Our regular visits to him sparked brief hopes for his future. However, it was short-lived. He unexpectedly appeared at our doorstep after expulsion for supposed boot theft while lacking proper clothing and creating turmoil in our household.

I secured a cable burial position with a contractor for Kent which gave him a second chance to redeem himself. I booked motel accommodations for him during his work period yet the harsh heat caused him to fall ill when he drank cold water after being exposed to high temperatures which resulted in him missing work. He left after working a week and left nothing behind except memories of disappointment.

Kent's latest message hit me with the force of a sudden thunderstorm. The message from the Drug and Alcohol Rehabilitation Center of Wichita Falls, Texas reached me and I was immediately filled with both concern and sorrow. The grim news revealed Kent had become intoxicated and was either arrested for public drunkenness or he had voluntarily entered the rehab center out of desperation.

While reading the letter memories of his laughter along with his youthful spirit and the dreams we shared for him filled my thoughts.

Understanding how the playful boy who enjoyed tree climbing and ball games became the man struggling with addiction proved difficult. My heart carried a deep sorrow when I remembered the unpredictable directions our lives had taken and those unexpected roads we journeyed. I dedicated myself to helping him overcome his challenges but we faced another difficult situation which added to his ongoing battle and left me feeling powerless.

Nearly twenty years passed without any communication between us, creating a divide filled with unresolved questions and concealed fears. I watched helplessly as Kent disappeared from my life like grains of sand slipping through my fingers and my dreams. The passage of time transformed days into weeks while weeks became months as the persistent feeling of loss defined every moment. My thoughts frequently drifted to his whereabouts and if he remained safe. My heart shattered when I pictured him alone in the world fighting his inner demons without my help.

In those years I endlessly revisited memories of our times together—the laughter at Jack in the Box and his determined gaze when he shared his future plans until those rare moments when I felt he had found his direction. The memories brought on deep regret while giving me a bittersweet sensation of past moments mixed with lost future possibilities. The silence persisted which taught me how to manage uncertainty while I maintained a hopeful expectation that Kent would one day contact me to confirm his well-being.

About a year and a half ago, a flicker of hope lit up my heart when I learned that Kent had shown up at the House of Peace, a church in Fort Worth. Just knowing he was in a place meant to help him brought a profound sense of relief, though it was short-lived. Soon, I found out that he had moved to Midlothian, Virginia, and my heart sank a little—wondering what awaited him there.

Judy Maxie from Midlothian, who ran a restaurant, sent Kent money for a bus ticket to her town. Kent moved in with Judy and her mother and worked as a cook at her restaurant during that period. Judy gave him an old pickup truck and then he searched throughout Midlothian for extra work opportunities. For a moment it seemed that Kent had established a stable life but hidden dangers remained at the edges of his fresh liberty. The bar at the restaurant which sold alcohol became a place where he started drinking beer again as a slow return to his old habits. His casual drinking quickly devolved into something much more damaging.

One fateful day, while under the influence of alcohol, Kent decided to drive the vehicle. He experienced devastating consequences after colliding with multiple vehicles while driving to his temporary residence. The news that the police arrested him for hit-and-run driving caused a tightening sensation in my chest. The phone call brought a weighty sadness as I thought about my son entangling himself again with bad decisions. I engaged Gray Gennings as Kent's lawyer for his trial because I wanted to provide him with all possible support during this difficult time. The court revoked his driver's license and imposed substantial fines while requiring him to report back to court. Kent did not follow through with his obligations and evaded both legal regulations and our aspirations for his rehabilitation. More than twelve months had passed since the devastating accident occurred.

Eventually, Kent received an opportunity to participate in an Arlington, Virginia program that helps people like him rebuild their lives. He remained in Midlothian because he required court permission to relocate. Gray Gennings offered his assistance once more as he helped Kent work through the complex bureaucratic processes.

After Kent obtained permission to depart, I arranged to send him bus money to Fort Worth via Judy because I eagerly awaited his return. Elation welled up inside me when he called me after returning to the House of Peace but was immediately challenged by my fears about what I might encounter. I drove quickly to Fort Worth while feeling apprehensive. I struggled to find his address which turned out to be harder than expected because my GPS malfunctioned and frustration welled up as I navigated through unfamiliar streets.

At last, I saw him standing before me but his appearance differed completely from the Kent I remembered. The vibrant energy of his younger days had disappeared. His face showed deep lines and gray hair along with a beard which revealed the challenges he had endured. As I opened my arms to hug him my heart fell but Kent only offered me a handshake instead. A weight settled on my world as I struggled with the emotional distance that became prominent between us over time.

We made our way to the closest Jack in the Box restaurant to talk because I wanted to find a way to reconnect through simple comforts. I provided him with money because I felt he needed financial support. Without hesitation he gave some of the money to Jack Yarbrough who operated the House of Peace. (We had a photo taken captured that moment as a small reminder of a long-awaited reunion we both needed.)

The moment we separated brought about a complicated blend of feelings within me. Seeing him again brought joy to my heart because he appeared to be enjoying his life as a H.O.P. worker traveling throughout the United States. Despite receiving many forms of support he remained unable to afford simple pleasures like a soda or snack. To provide him with some independence I mailed him a debit card loaded with $200. He requested the code from me so I sent it to him through text. When he returned from his journey he had only $75 left in his account which demonstrated that he lost control of life just as easily as he lost hope.

Writing this entry brings me sorrow because Kent has returned to the road without being able to access even basic comforts such as a cold beverage. Watching him battle this endless cycle feels suffocating because he seems unable to break free from it. Judy has kindly assisted him by providing a Home Depot reloadable debit card loaded with $200 because she understands his severe circumstances better than many others understand. I returned her money immediately, feeling relieved because someone cares for him but saddened by his current struggles.

As I sit down to write this, my heart feels heavy knowing Kent has returned to the road without being able to access even basic comforts such as a cold beverage. Watching him battle this endless cycle feels suffocating because he seems unable to break free from it. Judy has kindly assisted him by providing a Home Depot reloadable debit card loaded with $200 because she understands his severe circumstances better than many others understand. I returned her money immediately, feeling relieved because someone cares for him but saddened by his current struggles.

Kent's inability to manage even the little things creates a heavy burden in my heart. He may be physically present in the world, but the tools to truly make something of himself, to experience the small joys of life, are just out of reach. I often wonder what goes through his mind as he rides that endless road, how he feels when the sun beats down and he finds himself with pockets turned inside out, longing for just a few coins for a soda.

I am willing to help him whenever I can because I realize my support is just a small part of his larger battle. Through my actions I demonstrate that I care for him deeply regardless of the growing distance and immense challenges he faces. I wish to see him regain his stability. Every supportive action I take makes clear that he remains my son who deserves hope and connection for a brighter future. Through these tiny acts I hold onto the belief that he will eventually break free from his current struggles and rebuild his life.

*Chapter Eleven*

# Echoes of a Bright Light: Remembering Gene

We believed our hearts had reached their utmost limit from the pain of each miscarriage before life threw us yet another surprise. The long-awaited news arrived that Gracie was pregnant again and our hearts leaped with joy though tinged with nervous anticipation. The happiness we felt during this pregnancy was delicate yet intense because it showed how parenthood involves many unforeseen changes. As we prepared to enter this new phase we understood that our journey toward parenthood would be one filled with resilience and profound love that would establish our family's foundation on hope and strength. When Gene joined our family three years after our adoption of Kent he became a radiant source of happiness that looked toward a promising future. The moment I first held him in my arms I felt certain Gene would become an inspirational force in our family. The child exhibited boundless energy and innocence while displaying an intense curiosity comparable to a young explorer mapping uncharted territories. The sound of Gene's laughter filled our home with warmth and brought life and potential to our surroundings.

Our path to parenthood with Gene faced challenges starting when Gracie went into labor suddenly during an hour of adoration at Sacred Heart Church. At just seven months into her pregnancy she entered a fragile state which reflected the uncertainty we faced in all our prior pregnancies. Heartache and loss memories filled the room as the fears of miscarriage lingered but the doctor chose a cesarean section to give our baby a fighting chance.

Gene entered the world on March 27, 1963 as a premature infant weighing only 4 pounds and 4 ounces and appeared as a fragile being that took my breath away. I observed him inside the incubator and experienced a powerful mix of affection and trepidation. Watching him attempt to lift his tiny body from a wet diaper proved to be a defiant act against his fragile life. Panic took hold when he turned blue and I watched in horror as the nurse drew the blinds to hide the ensuing chaos from me. Gene experienced a terrifying oxygen deprivation because of an incubator malfunction. Relief washed over me when the equipment was repaired and Gene regained stability after my heart had raced.

After two weeks Gene finally came home to us, and I discovered he was small enough to fit in my hand. The way my wedding ring wrapped around his small arm demonstrated the love that encircled him.

Our father-and-son connection strengthened and flourished as he reached maturity. Gene exhibited shyness during social interactions but would join me on errands where he would stand with pride on my truck seat as an eager adventurer. I laugh every time I remember how I braked abruptly and saw him fall to the floor under the dashboard without being able to stop him.

Gene was an extraordinary child who illuminated every space with his insatiable curiosity. Gene's curious nature reminded me of that of a playful kitten with endless enthusiasm for exploration and discovery. His irresistible compulsion to push every button he found reflected his deep need to uncover the secrets of his environment. I frequently brought him to the telephone office so he could play with the equipment while I completed my work.

However, his desire to play often led him into dangerous predicaments. The recollection of him falling from the moving ladder inside the equipment room to the harsh tiled floor continues to haunt me. The event sent my heart into shock but his excited claim of "seeing stars" after looking up dazed yet unbroken showed his resilient spirit. His investigation resulted in a costly mistake when he turned off the main power source in the battery room triggering a police visit the next day to report that the office building had no electricity. The dial equipment operated throughout the entire night on batteries but experienced failure when morning arrived. Gene persistently searched for new experiences and adventures no matter what risks were involved.

I felt grateful as life regained its balance while Gene continued to grow stronger. Despite the return of happiness to our home life, Gracie entered a severe personal struggle. The urgent call I received still haunts my memory as I heard "Come" in trembling breaths. I reached her bedside only to discover her in a dire condition with hollowed eyes while she fought for survival. I ordered the doctor to get a second opinion while my heart raced with fear and desperation. Her health improved rapidly following surgery which exposed intestinal adherence to her cesarean scar while my love for her grew stronger each time I observed her healing process.

Gene possessed limitless energy and curiosity which drove him to explore beyond the boundaries of his universe. When Gene stopped showing his usual energy at age four I took him to Odessa Morrison who thought he had scarlet fever. I entered the doctor's office feeling downhearted but was hurt when the receptionist callously instructed me to "Just take your seat and wait your turn."

For years, Gene battled with tonsillitis. The persistence of his condition meant Gene had to wait until he reached the appropriate age to receive necessary tonsil surgery. In the course of three months when he reached his fifth birthday I had taken him to the doctor for medical attention 17 times. I experienced endless cycles of hope and disappointment during each medical appointment while carrying the emotional burden of parenthood.

At last we received a piece of good news. After checking his throat the doctor said that this was the best condition he'd ever seen it. We received the news about the tonsil removal just one day before the weekend started—when we believed we were close to finding relief.

A fresh wave of vigor washed over Gene when he recovered after his surgery making his transformation a delightful sight for everyone around him. His newfound energy was so remarkable that we jokingly said we might need to put his tonsils back in to prevent him from bouncing off the walls! We were relieved to see our little boy free from pain and living life to its fullest once more.

The next morning Gene showed off his restored energy following surgery which filled everyone with happiness. His post-surgery energy was so incredible that we joked about putting his tonsils back to prevent him from bouncing off the walls! Seeing our little boy return to joyful living without pain brought us great relief.

My heart overflowed with pride as time passed and I watched him grow into the person he became through our shared challenges. During Darlene Lueb's wedding festivities our excitement grew until Gene contracted chickenpox. He was scheduled to serve as the ring bearer at Darlene Lueb's wedding. I had to leave him by himself at home for brief times while I ran quick errands only six blocks distant. The wedding day came and brought me immense relief when Gene won his battle with chickenpox and his spots disappeared right before the ceremony. Even though he was alone at home I trusted his ability to handle himself responsibly so I told him to call me if he needed assistance. I attempted to call him but met with nothing more than an absolute quiet. A wave of fear surged through me as I ran home while my thoughts churned with concern. He looked at peace playing in his room while completely engrossed in his fantasy world. His response "I was too busy playing" demonstrated Gene at his best, who always led with his heart while remaining oblivious to the world's troubles.

He revealed his gentle nature when he bravely confessed to being unable to tell time at kindergarten and believed the sun and bird songs meant he was running late. The innocence he displayed made my heart feel heavy with emotion. He consistently concealed his challenges from others while carrying all difficulties personally despite his anxiety about sharing even minor problems.

My memory preserved these milestones as sacred rituals which imprinted themselves deeply. The day he had his first communion at Sacred Heart Church was memorable for him when he wore his scapular medal with pride. The man always wore his medal without removing it even on the night when he died tragically. We honored him with a breakfast gathering following Mass and surrounded ourselves with family and friends who held him dear.

During his high school years when computers were widespread yet our school had not adopted them Gene started fundraising to help Sacred Heart acquire computers. He devoted his after-school hours to tutoring classmates which demonstrated his generous nature. I admired Gene's intelligence and work ethic but felt concerned because his principal failed to recognize his skills. A nun secretly brought Gene back to school after closing so he could teach his classmates away from official supervision.

Gene exhibited his peculiar development at his home environment. The happiness in his eyes during the potato planting session showed our shared delight in understanding nature and witnessing growth magic. Memories of him protecting our garden from potato bugs remain vivid as he proclaimed his triumph by comparing himself to the Orkin man.

These myriad memories carry with them a haunting ache in my heart. Gene embodied far more than childhood because his spirit brought love and laughter while giving our lives direction. Each shared moment becomes more precious to me as I reflect on them because they remain forever woven into our family's beautiful memory tapestry—woven in unison yet now irrevocably changed.

Gene possessed a gentle nature which combined with his shyness to make him fade into the background yet he maintained a quiet depth that belonged only to him. At age ten he declared his independence by stating he no longer required a babysitter. Gracie consistently prepared breakfast meals which she would leave to bake before she went to work in the mornings. Gene demonstrated his responsibility by turning on the oven so that when we returned home for lunch we were welcomed by a delicious aroma which showed his growing maturity.

He succeeded in cooking our meals while keeping the house exceptionally clean with no mess remaining. His actions showed that he grasped how essential it was to create tranquility and structure within the disorderly family setting. It didn't take long before Gene took on yard duties with great enthusiasm as he mowed the grass and trimmed the edges perfectly.

Gardening became a shared passion between us, a quiet connection in which we could bond over the simple joys of nurturing life from the soil. He adored spending time by my side, digging in the earth, planting seeds, and watching them grow. Those moments were filled with laughter and learning, as he learned the beauty of patience and the rewards that nature would generously bestow. Gene's willingness to take on these responsibilities showcased not only his maturity but also the love and dedication he carried for our home and family.

Through gardening we developed a shared passion that allowed us to connect quietly while reveling in the basic pleasures of cultivating life from the earth. He cherished the moments together when we dug the earth and planted seeds before watching them grow. Moments with him teaching him to appreciate nature's patient gifts filled with joyous learning and laughter. Through Gene's readiness to accept these duties he demonstrated both his maturity and the deep love and commitment he had for our family and home.

Even though his actions often created chaos he brought joy and laughter to our lives. On November 25th each year my heart breaks as I recall how Gene left us before his time. A drunk driver took Gene's life in a tragic accident at the north edge of Sanger, Texas. The blockades in Muenster for the 2003 Christmas parade became a poignant contrast to the somber fact of his burial at Sacred Heart Cemetery. The funeral Mass for him took place at Immaculate Conception Church in Denton where he had married Kaylynn Paterson three years before. He never realized his dream of starting a family before his 40th birthday despite his intense longing for it.

*Chapter Twelve*

# Cherished Remembrances: Honoring Gene and Gracie

There is a solitary image of Gracie in my mind as she sat quietly in her lounge chair with the fading light of the sun on her face. It reflected a bittersweet nostalgia, a feeling I found familiar as we both often thought about Gene's passing.

Gene developed into a healthy child whose contagious laughter brought light and happiness to our home. Gracie watched in awe as he evolved from a delicate newborn into an energetic youngster who seemed to overflow with life and curiosity. His ability to overcome challenges transformed her fears into feelings of love and pride. Through her reflections she wanted to share her treasured recollections about him in my book The Way It Was which highlighted Gene's true nature and the happiness he created in her life. As we remembered the small joys that made our lives whole, our hearts both ached and expanded because those memories held both deep loss and the transforming power of love. The simplest experiences mattered most like feeling his warm hand against ours standing proudly as a ring bearer at a wedding and seeing him come home from school full of stories about his day's adventures.

One lighthearted yet touching memory that was a favorite of Gracie's was Gene at the breakfast table the day he started kindergarten, his small hands trembling slightly around his bowl. He suddenly began to cry. Concern swept over Gracie and me as we rushed to his side, asking him what was wrong. Through his tears, Gene confessed with a quivering voice, "I do not know how to learn." My heart ached at his vulnerability; the weight of expectation felt heavy on his young shoulders. We knelt beside him, doing our best to soothe his worries. "That's exactly why you're going to school," I gently reassured him. "School is where you learn all the things you're curious about." In that moment, I recognized that we were not just sending him off to a place of learning; we were helping him open the door to a new adventure, one filled with discovery and growth. Little did I know, this would be just the beginning of a lifelong journey of learning, exploration, and wonder for our sweet boy.

This was also around the time when a subtle change rippled through Gene's and Gracie's relationship. To Gracie's surprise, he started calling her "Mother" instead of the familiar "Mama." This transformation brought warmth to her heart, a sweet validation of his growing independence and maturity. His use of "Mother" became a term of endearment that she cherished deeply. It was a reminder of the bond they shared, and she relished every time he used it, feeling a sense of pride in his growth. Though he eventually transitioned to calling her "Mom," that fond title of "Mother" lingered for a while, serving as a bookmark in the precious story of his childhood—a time filled with the wonder of new beginnings and the bittersweet beauty of growing up.

As for me, Gene's little morning routine before he left for school consisted of kissing me and wrapping his little arms around me in a snug embrace. The simple pleasure of him always calling me "Dad" never failed to make my heart swell.

One of our most cherished moments of Gene's childhood were the ones when Gracie sang to him during bedtime. The way that Gene would light up as she sang was simply magical. Gracie's voice would fill the room like a warm blanket of melody. Gene would listen with wide eyes, enthralled by the playful notes of Gracie's songs. It was their special mother-son ritual, a time when all the worries of the world seemed to melt away, replaced by the simple joy of singing to him and the bond they shared.

Then one day, as Gracie lost herself in a song, Gene made a playful gesture, his little hand landing gently on Gracie's chest. With a mischievous grin, he loudly declared that he was turning off the radio. Gracie's laughter bubbled up in her voice as she replayed their bedtime scene to me. I could see how the innocence of that moment wrapped around her heart. It was a perfect blend of childhood wisdom and humor.

When Gene was little, he spent his days at Sylvia Hofbauer's daycare, where he found a second home filled with laughter and friendship. He thrived in that environment, and it was easy to see why—his playful spirit and gentle nature made him a favorite among the other children. Even after he started school, he would make it a point to stop by the daycare on his way to the telephone office, drawn to the familiar faces and the joy of playtime.

One day, wanting to ensure he wasn't getting in Sylvia's way during her busy hours, Gracie decided to call her. As soon as she mentioned sending Gene along to work with her, her voice resonated with warmth. "Oh, I like having him here," she replied affectionately. "He plays so well with the other children, and they really enjoy his company." Her words filled Gracie with pride, knowing that Gene, with his innate kindness, was making connections and spreading happiness wherever he went. It was a testament to the wonderful spirit he embodied, bringing joy to those around him, even in the simplest of places.

Gene's spirit truly shone when he played little league baseball, his excitement palpable each time he stepped onto the field. One season, he took on the role of right fielder, but as fate would have it, few balls flew in his direction. As the game unfolded, Gene's attention began to wander. Bored, he found himself mesmerized by the dance of birds soaring overhead, the flutter of leaves in the wind, and the subtle beauty of the world around him.

Noticing Gene's distraction from the game, I couldn't help but make my way over, concern showing all over my face. "Gene, you need to pay attention," I urged, wanting to keep him engaged and focused. The serious tone my voice prompted Gene to respond, a hint of exasperation lacing his small frame. "Dad, don't do that again," he said earnestly. I stood firm, reminding him that if he let his gaze drift once more, he would indeed have to step in again.

One evening during a little league game in Muenster, the atmosphere was electric, and as Gracie arrived, she spotted Gene bounding toward her, a look of distress on his face. To Gracie's surprise, the back of his uniform was torn. Without hesitation, she pulled out her trusty needle and thread, always kept handy for such emergencies, and led him back to the school bus. In those small moments—distracted by birds or mending a uniform—we could see the essence of Gene's youthful exuberance, a reminder of how quickly childhood flies by and how cherished those memories would always be.

<center>~~~~~~</center>

Although Gene loved baseball with intense enthusiasm, his greatest love remained the exhilarating experience of fishing together with me. The serene moments he spent fishing by the water's edge attracted him more than any sport played on the field. He made the tough decision to leave the team with a heavy heart but strong determination, which took both his coach and teammates by surprise. His coach made repeated efforts to convince him to remain on the team claiming that his potential to perform was unaffected by his absence from practice sessions. Gene's firm belief in fairness and integrity prevented him from playing because he knew it would be unfair to his teammates who attended every practice. Gene exhibited at a young age a deep understanding of responsibility and team spirit which shaped his entire life.

Gene experienced freedom after finalizing his decision when he took his fishing pole to make new meaningful memories with me. He valued the moments spent fishing more than any baseball trophy because they brought him joy through casting lines together and sharing conversations by the water's edge while anticipating each catch. True happiness manifested for Gene during those peaceful moments when we stood together enjoying life's simple pleasures.

One afternoon, the ever-energetic Gene was just a little guy, when Greg Gieb came over to play. While they were playing, something happened between the two that none of us saw coming, and in a moment of frustration we saw Gene wrap his tiny arms around Greg's waist and bit him. We were all shocked and even both boys were themselves confused. Gracie felt the need to address Gene's unexpected outburst. She took a deep breath and sat Gene down for a conversation to help him understand the kind of behavior that was not acceptable. Her voice was firm, yet filled with compassion as she explained the importance of expressing one's feelings without becoming aggressive. I could see the seriousness of Gracie's words sinking in, as the once innocent look on Gene's face visibly turned to that of a mixture of guilt and regret.

Once their talk was over, Gracie urged Gene to take responsibility for his actions and to go next door to the Giebs' house to apologize to Greg. Despite his hesitation, Gene walked up to the Giebs' door. We could sense his little heart racing. There was something about his eyes that showed that it mattered to him to make things right. I saw Gracie look at Gene with pride as he knocked and offered his apology. It was a defining moment for Gene, a small but important step in learning accountability. Seemingly ordinary happenings like that taught him lessons that would later shape him into the considerate person he was meant to become.

I think Gene was in fourth or fifth grade when he got into a fight with Alfred Hennigan. It came as a shock for both Gracie and me as Gene was not one to pick up fights. The Gene that everyone knew was sweet-natured and gentle, preferring to avoid conflict whenever possible. We later learned that his struggles with Alfred had been brewing for some time. Alfred seemed to have taken a special interest in pestering Gene during class with his constant teasing, making it impossible for Gene to focus on the lessons.

Gene's efforts of asking the teacher for a change of seating were refused, leaving him to endure Alfred's relentless annoyance. Then, one fateful day, after an especially trying class for Gene, he reached his breaking point. After school, he finally mustered enough courage to fight back, surprising everyone—including himself—by physically confronting Alfred. The incident quickly escalated, and it wasn't long before Alfred's mother came to the school, resulting in consequences for Gene. That evening, Gracie felt it was important for him to speak with me about what had happened. Gene was obviously reluctant and ashamed. We sat down and talked it through, both Gracie and I lecturing on the complexities of friendship in a language that the young Gene would be able to understand. Patiently Gracie explained to him that perhaps Alfred was just trying to reach out to him in the only way he knew how. Maybe he just wasn't aware of the boundaries he was crossing, she said. I could see that Gene was full of questions but tried hard to grasp what his parents were trying to teach him.

Years later, it was heartwarming to see how Gene's and Alfred's relationship evolved. They became good friends as if nothing happened.

I could not forget that one afternoon when we ventured out to Eisenhower Park at Lake Texoma for a fishing trip. I saw in Gene's sparkling eyes how excited he was as we settled down by the lake, fishing rods at the ready.

While the others cast their lines, hoping for a bite, it soon became obvious that luck was not on their side. Hours passed, but not a single fish took the bait. Just as Gene started getting disappointed, his rod suddenly bent, and there was a strong tug from beneath the surface. With wide eyes, he sprang into action, as he pulled his rod with all his strength. I watched in awe as Gene wrestled with the line, his laughter mingling with shouts of excitement and triumph. The struggle seemed to last forever, but Gene was determined. And then it happened—the water erupted as Gene reeled in a magnificent fish, its scales glinting like jewels in the sunlight. While others looked on with envy, amazed by Gene's catch, a wave of pride washed over me and Gracie. We couldn't help but beam at our son, whose grin was wide from ear to ear. That was an unforgettable moment for us, a joyful testimony to Gene's patience and tenacity, as well as his ability to turn an ordinary fishing trip into an extraordinary adventure we would treasure forever.

Our boys never had the chance to know their Friske grandparents, and Gracie always felt like it was a gap in our family's story. The connection that should have existed between generations was absent. It wasn't just that the boys didn't know them; it was also the indifference that seemed to flow from their grandparents, a lack of engagement that felt like a missed opportunity to build cherished memories.

As Gracie watched them navigate childhood without that familial bond from her side, she couldn't help but feel a profound sadness for all the stories untold and laughter unshared. It was a relationship that might have flourished but instead remained a distant, unfulfilled dream, a reminder of what could have been.

I remember a time many years ago when buying a Coke meant having a cool glass bottle in your hand, each one guaranteeing refreshment and an incentive of getting your five cents returned back to you. In our home, we had this rule: the Coke bottles were not to be cashed in for quick change. Instead, she'd be the only one allowed to collect them after they were emptied and bring them back to the grocery store on her next grocery trip to buy more Coke. Somehow it inculcated a sense of responsibility in our boys.

But one Saturday, just before Mother's Day, Gracie wondered where all her empty Coke bottles had gone to. She interrogated Gene and Kent, none of whom confessed what they did with the Coke money, which concerned her. Much to her dismay, she soon was able to put two and two together that they had taken the bottles to cash them in for some pocket change.

When Mother's Day came, Gracie was taken by surprise when the two boys presented her with a carefully wrapped gift that looked really special. Shen then realized that they had used the Coke money to buy her a special Mother's Day present. Gracie couldn't help feeling guilty for fussing over the lost Coke money when clearly their intention was nothing but sweets, which warmed her heart. At that moment all her frustrations were replaced by love and appreciation of her thoughtful boys. She told me later how she felt profoundly blessed to be their mother.

Gracie and I shared an excited anticipation as we organized our eagerly awaited Hawaiian vacation to the tropical paradise offering sun-soaked beaches and relaxed afternoons. As the trip approached I vividly imagined walking on warm sand and feeling salty breezes touch my hair. One afternoon changed our joyful expectation when Gene entered the room looking visibly upset after school.

He remained standing before us as his disappointment washed over him while he explained that during the Friday night game each player would present their mothers with a rose which he had eagerly awaited. When I realized we would miss witnessing that moment my heart dropped and I saw the pain clear in his eyes. The thought of Gene feeling let down during this special occasion compelled me to reconsider our plans because I didn't want his sadness.

Gracie and I shared a moment of silent understanding through our connected glance. We decided without hesitation that the Hawaiian adventure needed to be cut short. The love we felt for our son became more important than our plans for a vacation. We quickly revised our travel schedule and rushed home to ensure we didn't miss this important event.

When we reached our destination late Friday my mind swirled with elation and relief. We arrived just in time and when Gene proudly presented the rose to Gracie her radiant face warmed my heart. The moment evolved into a precious family memory which reinforced the idea that family love surpasses any exotic vacation destination.

## *Chapter Thirteen*

# From Here to Everywhere

Our shared passion for exploring new destinations has always helped me and Gracie strengthen our connection and build unforgettable memories together. Our travels took us from quaint seaside villages to bustling urban centers where every trip became an exciting adventure that brought us pure happiness and amazement. Evenings were spent either planning our future adventures or reflecting on past journeys while excitement surged between us like a sparkling champagne toast welcoming our future travels.

### *The Great Earthquake in California*

Our California journey from 1989 stands out as a vivid memory in my mind. We were to attend the U.S.T.A. National Convention, filled with anticipation for new experiences. Upon arriving in San Francisco, we checked into the multitowered Hilton, and I instinctively requested a non-smoking room on a lower floor, my mind still nagged by whispers of an impending earthquake. To my dismay, we were assigned to the 12th floor of Tower No. 3, the oldest section of the hotel. After a day of meetings, I returned to our room, eager to relax with my shoes off and watch the World Series, while Gracie lounged nearby, happily dressed in her slip after a long day.

Just as I settled in, the room began to tremble, gently at first, then with increasing violence. Gracie asked, "What's happening?" I reassured her, "I believe we are having an earthquake." Not for a moment did I truly think it could happen. But the shaking escalated into a frantic upheaval, the walls echoing the building's groans. In those critical seconds, I pondered whether we were safer inside our room or in the basement with 47 stories looming above us. Gracie urged me to catch the television set, which was on the brink of toppling out of the cabinet.

As we fled our room, the fire alarms blared, urging us to evacuate. We dashed down the stairwell illuminated by flickering battery-powered lights, joining a growing crowd of guests heading for safety. Emerging from the building into the chaos of the street, we learned of the extensive damage caused by the earthquake. Despite being situated in an earthquake-proof building, it struck me how quickly life can change. As we took in the aftermath, I couldn't help but wonder if we would ever return to San Francisco. While the experience left me with resilient appreciation for our safety, Gracie felt she'd had enough of the city for a while.

## Nova Scotia

Gracie and I had an unforgettable journey through Nova Scotia. The moment I set foot in Halifax I found myself captivated by its stunning natural beauty and inviting charm. A scenic bus journey along breathtaking coastlines brought us to Lunenburg's historic streets and then to the renowned Cabot Trail where the rugged landscape met the Atlantic Ocean dramatically.

Our vacation included frequent meals of local specialties such as fresh mussels and renowned scallops which we enjoyed on the scenic waterfront. Our trip's most memorable experience included visiting the Alexander Graham Bell National Historic Site in Baddeck. Exploring the history of communication technology and viewing the industry-defining inventions triggered personal career memories in telecommunications.

The quaint fishing village of Mahoney Bay became our final destination where we visited Amos Pewter to appreciate the skilled craftsmanship on display. The warmth and hospitality from the locals turned our journey into a remarkable experience and understanding the Acadian people's rich history allowed me to develop a stronger bond with the area.

The departure from Nova Scotia prompted me to think about both the happiness we experienced and the friendships we formed with other travelers. The adventure stands out as a treasured memory because it showed me how exploration creates powerful bonds and unforgettable moments shared with Gracie.

## *Our Mediterranean Cruise*

After being dropped off by Joey Anderson at DFW Airport, Gracie and I eagerly began our journey. We boarded what appeared to be a late-model 747, complete with four engines and an upstairs passenger compartment, all aboard a British Airways flight to London. Our Business Class seats were certainly a new experience for us. I found myself in a window seat, boxed in and needing to crawl over the feet of the passenger facing me in the aisle, which meant I was flying backward. Gracie, seated next to me with a view of the window between us, had her own challenges, as the passenger in front of her frequently needed to climb over her feet to get to their seat.

The flight to London was uneventful until we arrived at Heathrow Airport, where we sat on the tarmac for about an hour while waiting for our connecting flight to Venice. We were fortunate that an attendant helped us secure seats on the next flight at Gatwick. He also provided us with express bus tickets to get there quickly. However, when we arrived at the bus stop, it became clear there was a hold-up, and time was running short. Without hesitation, I hailed a taxi and watched in disbelief as the meter climbed—over £88 by the time we reached the airport, but I was relieved to hand the driver a $100 bill, seeing the satisfaction on his face.

Once we reached Venice, we quickly retrieved our luggage and passed through customs, where a Viking agent greeted us. He took care of our bags—the last time we would have to handle them, thanks to the excellent service provided by Viking. After gathering the rest of our group, we boarded a medium-sized bus that took us to the ship, which was located in an area of Venice far from the business district and popular sightseeing spots.

When we boarded, we received our cabin keys and navigated through the ship to our third-floor suite, located at the end of a long hallway. Opening the door revealed a sitting room that led to a bedroom and a spacious bathroom, complete with a walk-in closet. The highlight was a shower and a large bathtub in their own enclosure, featuring a picturesque window and blinds for privacy.

Our balcony wrapped around the corner of the ship, offering stunning views and a unique vantage point from which we could see straight into the window of our bathtub.

The ship had various amenities—just one level down from our cabin was the elegant dining room where we usually had dinner, while breakfast was served in the buffet area on the seventh floor. We spent time exploring the ship, which boasted a large central sitting area with live music and a theater that featured entertainment each night. With 900 passenger cabins, we were thrilled to be aboard a vessel rich with activity and experiences waiting to unfold. It promised to be an adventure of a lifetime.

## Peru

In 2015, Gracie and I embarked on an incredible adventure known as the Grand European River Cruise, beginning with a journey across several enchanting countries. Our trip kicked off in Amsterdam, where we boarded a spacious ship, excited to see what awaited us. From the moment we stepped on board, the excitement was palpable; we were surrounded by fellow travelers eager to explore Europe's breathtaking sites.

During our time in Europe, we visited various cities, each boasting cobblestone streets, majestic old churches dating back to the 13th century, and charming sidewalk cafés where we could enjoy refreshing beer. Although many places shared these common features, there were unique experiences along the way. In Amsterdam, we took a scenic cruise through the picturesque canals, concluding our ride at the world-renowned Van Gogh Museum, home to the largest collection of his masterpieces.

We made our way through Germany, exploring the stunning Gothic Cathedral in Cologne—an architectural marvel that survived the ravages of World War II—before travelling to Mainz, where I was reminded of my time in the service years ago. The stop at the Gutenberg Museum opened my eyes to the important history of printing and reading that had shaped our world.

As we continued, we journeyed through the scenic landscapes of the Main and Danube Rivers, marveling at the beauty of the surrounding nature and visiting quaint villages. Highlights included our visit to Nuremberg, where I had served as a prison guard in the infamous Palace of Justice—an eerily powerful reminder of history.

Each day brought new adventures, from enjoying a delightful picnic lunch to listening to an exceptional organ concert in Passau. In Vienna, we attended a concert featuring the works of Mozart and Strauss, feeling the rhythm and energy of the city come alive. Another memorable stop was Bratislava, Slovakia, where we took a mini-train ride through the city and visited the stunning St. Martin Cathedral.

Finally, we reached Budapest, Hungary, where the Danube River gracefully divided the historic Buda Hills from the sleek boulevards of Pest. We immersed ourselves in the city's vibrant culture, enjoying a visit to a diamond factory and tasting the local cuisine. As the cruise came to a close, we gathered for a Captain's dinner, cherishing the connections we had made with fellow travelers, especially Jim and Felicia Jones from Round Rock, Texas, whose company made the experience even more enjoyable.

After disembarking from the Viking Pride, we spent an extra night in the Budapest Hilton, where we attended Mass at St. Pious Church. Though the service was conducted in Hungarian, I felt a sense of familiarity in the Latin prayers, bridging the gap between cultures.

As I reflect on this incredible journey through Europe, I realize how fortunate Gracie and I were to share these experiences. The landscapes, cultures, and people we encountered added depth to our lives and strengthened our bond—a reminder that love and adventure go hand in hand.

## *Portugal*

When we left DFW at 4: At 10 p.m., I experienced both excitement and tiredness. Our plane landed in Frankfurt at 9 a.m. local time after nine hours and fifty-five minutes of intense flying. The plane seats did recline but offered minimal comfort and I could only manage brief sleep despite trying hard. After a three-hour layover, we boarded another Lufthansa flight to Lisbon, arriving at around 3: By 3:30 p.m., I was completely wiped out from the extended travel.

Once we disembarked from the Lisbon plane, Viking River Cruises' van was ready to transport us directly to our accommodation at the Trivial Hotel. We promptly checked into our room where we freshened up before completely collapsing into bed due to 24 hours of insufficient sleep. Our bodies aged but we stayed functional until we realized a short sleep break became essential for us.

We found a hearty buffet breakfast ready for us in the morning to fuel our half-day exploration of Lisbon. We collected our vox receivers which allowed us to listen to our guide before beginning our adventure. We visited Belem first where we admired the stunning Jeronimos Monastery which holds UNESCO World Heritage designation. The stunning architecture that we viewed set a high standard for our entire tour. We went uphill through the twisting

Bairro Alto streets where Lisbon's diverse history surrounded us before descending through Alfama to reach the city's waterfront.

After checking out of our hotel we took a scenic bus ride to Porto where signs to the famous town of Fatima caught our attention and made me wish we had visited that place. We stopped first in Coimbra where Portuguese kings were born and which houses an ancient European university before we took a lunch break to continue our travel.

We reached Porto at noon and proceeded to Vila Nova de Gaia to reach the dock. The Viking ship known as "Douro" exemplified beauty while being specifically designed for the Douro River's distinctive features. Terraced vineyards leading to the Atlantic and the stunning river views left me completely breathless. Upon locating our cabin after boarding the ship we recognized it as the tiniest cabin we had ever stayed in yet it maintained a cozy feel with a practical design and a surprisingly nice bathroom.

The ship provided accommodations for approximately 120 passengers and we soon familiarized ourselves with its layout including the lounge area for relaxation. Whenever we left the ship we got onto our designated buses which were marked as Bus A for our group. Our vox units proved extremely convenient because they enabled free exploration while keeping us in touch with our guide at all times.

The cobblestone streets of Portugal demanded physical stamina for navigation which we managed well thanks to our consistent exercise routine at home. The evening meals with our English retired couple friends turned into cherished moments filled with laughter and shared stories.

Our Porto visit reached a peak when we toured the port wine-making facility followed by an extraordinary lunch in Salamanca where we enjoyed a flamenco performance amidst the historical ambiance of a UNESCO site. The site displayed a captivating blend of historical and modern elements through its impressive Gothic architectural design.

My exploration of local villages such as Facaios taught me about their traditional bread-making techniques. I bought a Moscatel wine bottle from a picturesque local shop with excitement but later discovered we had left it on the bus. The thought of losing my treasured item caused my heart to plummet.

The stunning vistas of dramatic rock formations alongside terraced grapevine-covered hills kept my adventurous spirit driving me forward. During our departure preparations on our final night I experienced a small stroke of luck as my forgotten wine was returned to me bringing sweetness to our mixed emotions of farewell.

Our return trip to Dallas brought both exhaustion and gratitude as I reflected on our exploration of Portugal's historic landscapes. The people who charmed us along with spectacular views and the impressive locks we encountered on the Douro River made this journey unforgettable.

## Russia

The idea of visiting Russia had been a long-held dream for Gracie and me because we wanted to explore how people lived in a nation once wrapped in mystery and political ideology. The "People to People Ambassador Program" which President Eisenhower started gave us our initial chance to visit Russia in 1965. We had to decline participation because our children were too young to stay by themselves for an extended period.

The following February 1986 we discovered a Russian tour organized by the National Telephone Cooperative Association. We eagerly enrolled in the Russian tour since our boys had reached an age where they could look after themselves. We had to fly to New York first because direct flights to Russia didn't exist at that time. We encountered fellow tourists with similar interests in Russia which generated high anticipation among us during our meeting.

However, fate had other plans. Our plane experienced mechanical failure near the gate while we waited in the JFK International Airport lounge. The delay resulted in each passenger receiving a bar voucher which led us to discover the catastrophic Chernobyl nuclear disaster news broadcast on the television screen. The thought that our travel arrangements might face disruption weighed heavily upon us. We were bussed to a hotel in New York after discovering the flight's hydraulic steering hose would need to be flown in from Dallas. The televised coverage of the Chernobyl disaster made Gracie and me more worried about our trip as we watched it unfold that night. Our decision to avoid traveling to Russia proved to be prudent when we learned that many group members found the Russians unaware of the disaster.

Reflecting on our previous plans we have now found a Viking River Cruise that starts at Saint Petersburg and ends in Moscow. Our long-standing desire to visit Russia was rekindled by its enchanting appeal which led us to eagerly embrace this fresh journey.

Our arrival in Frankfurt followed an overnight flight from DFW which required us to make a quick dash through the airport to board our connecting Lufthansa flight to St. Petersburg. Petersburg. As we boarded the plane we rode a special bus which expanded its center section for smooth passenger entry and exit. As we drove through the rain to the airplane passengers packed into the bus with their carry-on luggage. I felt as though I stepped into another era when I descended from the outdoor stairs upon landing in Russia.

The St. Petersburg airport stood out as an outdated version of modern airports through its single baggage claim belt and its old-fashioned building structure. Once we collected our luggage we arranged a cab ride to reach our hotel. As our driver maneuvered through the disorderly traffic our appreciation grew for the driving culture where vehicles occupied every available space. It became obvious that the driver had lost his way when we arrived near our hotel. Our driver left us before a nondescript building that served as our hotel entrance identified by a tiny sign.

The online booking by Gracie gave us an unsettling first impression when we arrived at what seemed to be a warehouse. As we walked through the courtyard to enter the building we discovered that it housed a pleasant hotel with modern conveniences. After resting in our beautiful room we went out to explore the surrounding neighborhood.

We entered a small restaurant because we felt hungry but while sausage plates sounded good to order we hesitated over choosing drinking water. Our choice of Coke was incorrect because it contained local water. After considering our options we chose beer because it was the safer option. My cab fare took a large share of my Frankfurt ruble exchange which led us to look for a nearby bank.

We struggled to navigate Russian because many letters displayed in reverse order to our eyes. Our initial choice led us to the wrong place but a few steps away we located the proper bank where we changed our dollars to rubles. Two well-dressed young men approached us on our return to the hotel and asked to take our photo. The two well-dressed young men who offered to take our picture were Seventh Day Adventists from the USA who were conducting missionary work in Russia and they showed great enthusiasm for conversation.

We reached our destination one day before our actual trip to adjust to the new time zone. We boarded a bus bound for the famous Hermitage Museum after breakfast the next day. The Hermitage Museum holds Russia's most esteemed art collection which includes over 2.7 million exhibits displayed like treasures within its walls. The prospect of viewing works from Da Vinci and Michelangelo alongside Van Gogh left me completely awestruck.

When we reached the destination we joined other visitors as each tour guide displayed signage for their respective groups. The museum's intense heat and stuffiness drove me to find open windows for fresh air. My favorite exhibit featured the magnificent carriages used by Catherine the Great which highlighted both the opulence and difficulties of travel during an era of terrible road conditions.

The museum located inside the Winter Palace serves dual roles as both an art gallery and a historical monument.

The start of our new adventure brought immense satisfaction as we explored the country I had long wished to visit. The gentle sound of water against our Viking ship combined with the Neva River created a tranquil setting which stood in stark contrast to St. Petersburg's vibrant city life that we had left behind. Petersburg.

The Russian landscape revealed itself as we glided along the river. The appearance of large apartment buildings instead of single-family homes caught my attention as it demonstrated how historical factors have molded living conditions in this country. Observing locals performing ordinary tasks including riverbank fishing filled me with warmth as I watched these simple moments come to life.

While the ship offered comfort during our journey I started using my portable GPS to track our speed. Our steady upstream movement at five to six miles per hour allowed us to soak in our surroundings fully. I brought my laptop to maintain contact with my family members and friends from home. My AT&T phone functioned properly in Russia which enabled me to maintain contact within this mystical place.

Europe's largest lake, Lake Ladoga, became part of our navigation route during our voyage. The Svir River guided us toward Mandrogy where we experienced a traditional Russian life museum village setting. Visiting a vodka museum and purchasing handcrafted items were possible options there. Gracie and I decided to explore and experience the distinctive atmosphere.

The sun started its descent below the horizon while we made our way through the Volga-Baltic waterway that connects the Volga River to the Baltic Sea. The engineering behind our journey through this vast network of rivers and canals amazed me because our ship used locks to adjust its elevation throughout the trip.

Our trip reached a peak during our stop at Kuzino where we left the boat to tour the historic Kirillo-Belozersky Monastery. Saint Cyril established this remarkable building in 1397 where its thick walls appeared to narrate stories from numerous centuries. Our local guide led us through the monastery's walled area to show its wooden chapels and the magnificent Assumption Cathedral. The massive walls surrounding me created a profound sensation of moving through a tangible piece of history.

The display showcased many icons alongside gifts gifted by past tsars whose legacy remained palpable throughout the monastery. The artworks' exquisite craftsmanship left me in awe. Gracie and I spent some time with local children and artisans who displayed a sustained dedication to maintaining their traditional heritage which was very moving.

We went back to our ship after touring the monastery and experienced a scenic shift from historical austerity to colorful vibrancy during our meal. The beauty of the Russian countryside flowed past while reminding me of the nation's rich history and cultural layers.

On board our ship we enjoyed a performance of traditional Russian music and dance that evening. The music touched our hearts while the dancers expressed vivid tales through their movements. A remarkable experience allowed us to deeply engage with the local culture and we felt thankful for our involvement in it all.

The feeling of accomplishment settled over me when we reached Moscow. Our dream of visiting Russia became reality and we established meaningful connections while learning about its diverse way of life. Our cabin window offered me perspective on the vast distance between our original failure in 1986 and our current triumph. The passage of time had brought us to this moment where we stood embraced by the heart of Russia. This journey transcended mere sightseeing and turned into an authentic personal exploration that demonstrated the power of perseverance and following dreams.

My perception of Russia was shifting from viewing it as an enigmatic and distant place to recognizing its stunning beauty and complex nature alongside its friendly people and untold stories. The opportunity to explore Moscow's renowned sights and dynamic culture filled us with excitement while we expressed gratitude for reaching the place that had intrigued us for years.

# Cuba

Our 59th wedding anniversary was drawing near and we, Gracie and I, wanted to mark the occasion with a special celebration. Upon finding out about a "Person to Person Tour" taking place in Cuba during our anniversary period it seemed like an ideal chance. Previous Collette tours had been enjoyable but this upcoming one promised a distinct experience. We possessed valid passports but obtaining a visa for Cuba added an extra element of anticipation to our trip.

The itinerary included flying to Miami for one night followed by a charter flight to Cuba. Preparing for our trip required us to ensure our luggage and carry-ons stayed below 44 pounds which led us to pack strategically.

Julian Hernandez drove us early on October 7 to the Gainesville First State Bank Conference Center where we encountered fellow travelers from our region. We picked up additional participants before reaching DFW International Airport where we completed our check-in with American Airlines. The plane had more than 200 passengers but we were fortunate to be seated next to the restrooms at row 33.

Once we landed in Miami and got our luggage we met our tour guide who was starting his initial journey with Collette. At night we met at a well-known Cuban eatery where we joined 12 tourists from Wisconsin and New York for a dinner.

Our tour guide provided us with essential travel instructions for our Cuba trip while we were in Miami. The special license obtained by Collette Travel Service permitted us to join educational exchange activities throughout our visit and provided reassurance. At all times we carried our authorization letter but Cuba authorities never checked for it which allowed us to explore Havana without any restrictions.

We started our next day with a hearty breakfast buffet followed by our bus trip to the airport. This trip our flight to Cuba operated through a King Air charter service. At the departure gate we nervously observed the weighing of our luggage followed by a meticulous check of our visas and passports. The charter flight we boarded unexpectedly turned out to be a Boeing 737 which had numerous vacant seats well above the established weight limits.

When we arrived in Havana the airport was packed and baggage claim felt chaotic with saran-wrapped packages adding to the disorder. Upon leaving customs we encountered our local guide who smoked heavily and possessed extensive knowledge about Havana yet whose name we failed to remember. We stepped onto a compact Chinese bus that drove us through Havana's streets for 45 minutes while I observed the striking contrast between lively inhabitants and deteriorating buildings.

The modern Hotel Quinta Avenida Habana offered a refreshing relief but its dusty carpets showed they lacked proper cleaning equipment. The absence of Internet service led me to leave my computer behind as I saw guests congregating in a particular lobby area to try and find some form of connectivity.

We dined at Divina Pastora Restaurant while watching Havana and its harbor but Gracie faced difficulty picking from their extensive fish menu. Following dinner we experienced the Canonazo which involved nightly cannon firings in honor of Cuba's independence. As the powerful blast shook the windows it signaled an energetic start to our Cuban adventure.

We started our day with a hearty breakfast before taking a bus to Old Havana where we explored beautiful plazas and discovered the city's rich architecture only to be disappointed because the planned discussion about a local primary school never happened. We felt let down when none of our guides provided an official tour or education system insights. I made a stealthy attempt to look inside the Cathedral de la Habana but the guide walked on because religious sites didn't interest him.

Our group redirected our attention to Santovenia which operated as a Catholic charity for senior citizens. The dignity with which couples lived together was heartwarming but the reality was stark as they washed their laundry outdoors without any modern conveniences. The nun overseeing operations provided detailed information about their living conditions which demonstrated exceptional care management.

Our third day took us to the scenic Pinar del Rio region but we had to stop often due to bus problems during our journey to Vinales. The scenic surroundings made our journey rewarding while a tasty Cuban sandwich from a local restaurant preceded our visit to a tobacco farmer. Observing his demonstration of tobacco drying and cigar rolling gave us a genuine understanding of the local culture.

The Cuban people's challenges became apparent when farmers spoke English to share their stories about government officials collecting most of their income. The farmers maintained their strong spirit even though they lived in simple two-room flat-roofed homes.

Our evenings gained a delightful atmosphere from music and dancing experiences at several Havana restaurants after we returned to the city. We toured a daycare center and visited an Afro-Cuban location during our trip.

## Oklahoma City

Over several years Gracie and I planned a trip on the Heartland Flyer to Oklahoma City with our friends John and Mary Lou Leftwich. The long-awaited trip on Tuesday, November 15, 2011, became a reality at last. We could sense the intense anticipation when we reached the train station. Our train arrived late because a huge freight train with three engines blocked the track right before our scheduled departure. The passage of freight cars appeared endless with the unsettling noise of a particularly unstable car.

We finally detected our train's approach after waiting for approximately 25 minutes. The engineer used his loud whistle to signal the train's arrival through the night's silence. The conductor helped us board by putting a stool next to the train after it stopped.

The journey to Oklahoma City expected to last three hours turned into viewing our rear because the seats faced backward instead of the scenery ahead. The darkness outside limited our view to almost nothing. We asked the conductor about crossing the Red River Bridge but discovered we had already crossed it some time ago.

We experienced hunger and expected to eat during the train ride. We proceeded to the snack bar located one car ahead and descended some stairs. Gracie and I warmed our ham and cheese sandwiches from the snack bar then I added a cinnamon roll and a Diet Pepsi to complete my meal.

During the train ride to Oklahoma City it stopped multiple times at Ardmore and Purcell before slowing down at Pauls Valley. The church group which occupied our train car departed at Norman, Oklahoma. Upon arriving in Oklahoma City we descended the circular staircase searching for our luggage. Our bags were already placed aside for us by the conductor. We collected our things and moved toward the elevator as we prepared for the cold atmosphere because it was 45 degrees.

We checked into our accommodation at the Marriott located just one block from the train station. The eighth-floor room featured a king-sized bed in a handicapped-accessible space which was very pleasant.

After having a substantial breakfast early in the morning we proceeded to the trolley stop leading to the Oklahoma Museum about the Alfred P. Murrah Federal Building bombing. Murrah Federal Building by Timothy McVeigh.

During our arrival the Empty Chair Memorial created a solemn atmosphere. The empty chairs we saw when looking down symbolized every individual who died in the attack and served as a powerful reminder of the tragic event. We moved forward to encounter multiple wire fences displaying visitor mementos and memorials that showcased the deep effects of that tragic day. Our journey through the site became an emotional lesson that vividly displayed the historical importance of the events we saw.

<hr />

## Our Trip to Alaska and The Cruise
### (from Gracie's Perspective)

On June 29, 1992, we started our day at 4:30 a.m. We were going to Anchorage, Alaska, for the OPASTCO summer meeting. We left home at 5:30 a.m. to stop in Denton to pick up Gene to head for the airport. Alvin and I left DFW Airport on Delta Flight 1845 at 8:25 a.m. headed for Anchorage. Gene left on an American Airlines flight at 10:55 a.m. for Anchorage, also. The reason we did not go on the same flight is because we booked ours with our cruise.

We landed in Salt Lake City for a brief stop. We did not leave the airport. We arrived in Anchorage at 1:55 p.m. We rented a car while we waited for Gene's flight to arrive. We stayed at the Sheraton Anchorage Hotel. It is a really nice hotel. On one side is a cemetery, and on the other side there used to be the famous 5th Street, with all the call girls and a soup kitchen. The girls have gone, and the soup kitchen is a gift shop now. We were in room 732, and Gene was in room 722. On the evening we arrived at Josephine's in the hotel. It was a very nice and elegant restaurant. At 11:30 p.m. in June, it is like daytime in Anchorage; sunset comes at about 2 a.m. It never really got dark.

On Sunday, June 30th, we went to the 10 a.m. Mass at the Holy Family Cathedral. At 1:30 p.m. we boarded a bus for the Palmer golf course. Tee time was 4 p.m. All three of us played in the OPASTCO golf tournament, which was run rather loosely. They did not have any golf carts assigned, and some had to pull carts. It worked out okay, and everyone finally got started playing via a shotgun start. My team won second place and received a trophy. Alvin won an umbrella that was given away at the party after the tournament. While we were playing golf we had some of the most beautiful views anyone has ever seen.

On Monday, July 1st, we took the Anchorage City tour. In the afternoon we rested for a little while before we went to the OPASTCO reception in the evening.

On Tuesday we went to the General Sessions. We had lunch with John and Carolyn Rauh. In the afternoon the men went to the meetings, and Carolyn and I went shopping. I won a $100 travel certificate from Co-Bank. I signed up for the gift in their hospitality suite. That evening we all went to the Fred Follies banquet and show. It was a lot of fun.

On Wednesday we had the OPASTCO breakfast with John and Thelma Calendar. They are always so much fun. That afternoon we all attended different seminars. We had lunch with OPASTCO. The trip lasted through July 13th, and we had a lot of wonderful moments during our stay, particularly during our cruise.

On July 8th I entered the fashion show. While I was getting ready for the show, Alvin went to see the communications room on the ship. The Captain arranged for Alvin and some of the men on the cruise to do this. They missed my turn as a model. I modeled a hot pink jogging suit. I purchased a blue jogging suit. Later, we were on deck looking at many beautiful glaciers, as we were in Glacier National Park. We played ping pong and spent a lot of time on deck that day. After dinner w went to see "Cabaret Showtime" and "The Music Man." After the show we went to the casino but the machines did not pay off for us. Later we went to the midnight buffet-one thing about a cruise is that you get to eat a lot.

On Tuesday, July 9th, when we woke up the ship was rocking back and forth a little. I was looking in the mirror and could see that I was holding myself so as not to fall into the mirror, then, suddenly, holding myself because I was falling away from the mirror. My cosmetics never knew where they were; they kept shifting around.

Eventually, we docked at Skagway, left the ship and were told to return promptly at 6 p.m. We were told that if we were late, they would leave us. Skagway was a unique little town. We took the White Pass Railway tour, then, after the train ride, we walked all over town and ate in a little restaurant. Without tourists this town would dose down.

Later, we walked down to the telephone office. There were two employees in the office, and they were very friendly, showing us all around the place. They seemed to be a little more relaxed with their work than we were with ours. We returned to the shop on time, and after our evening meal we went to see the show "In the Mood." Before the show started we danced a little. It was kind of funny when we were dancing-sometimes when you lifted your foot it did not come down right because the ship was leaning one way or the other. After the show we visited the casino again, but, alas, our luck hadn't changed.

On Wednesday, July 10th, we docked at Juneau, the capital of Alaska. It appeared that the only way to get into the town was by boat. That morning, while Alvin was washing his hair, he wanted to use some hair conditioner. He reached for it, but instead picked up the bottle of Woolite instead. That gave us something to laugh about. Once we made it to shore we took a gold panning tour and found some gold. Later, we took the Taku Glacier Tour and then went up in a float plane that took us to the Taku Lodge for a salmon dinner. It was delicious. The scenery on the way back was very beautiful. The airplane flew very low over several glaciers, and I felt like I was in heaven-it was just gorgeous.

We returned to the ship at 5 p.m. After dinner we went to the show "Cabaret Showtime." The entertainment throughout the cruise was great, as good as any Las Vegas show. After dinner Alvin and I entered the "Twist Contest" before trying our hands at the casino once more. Our luck still hadn't changed.

After breakfast the next day we went to the horse races and won a little money. Then we went to the newlywed game. We entered but were not chosen to participate. We had an early lunch because we were going ashore at Ketchikan. We had to dock offshore and take a "tender" to shore and back. They really packed many people in these small people movers. It was kind of scary-I guess I will follow Alvin anywhere. It rained and rained-we got all wet. We took a tour but could not see much because of the rain. We returned to the ship at 6:30 p.m. for the formal dinner, after which we attended the show "Tin Pan Alley." Then we went to the Lip Sync show and paid another visit to the casino. Of course, our luck was the same. We attended the midnight buffet.

On Friday, our next to last day on the trip, we stayed on the ship all day. We were heading for Vancouver. It rained some more that day; in fact, it rained pretty much all day, making for a cool, yucky time on deck. We bet on the horse racing again and won a little. We played bingo and didn't win at all. We walked on the walking and jogging area on deck. Alvin purchased a gold watch. Another visit to the casino produced the usual results.

Because we were soon to leave the ship we packed that evening. It was hard to get everything back in the luggage. I think luggage grows when we travel. As our last dinner concluded we tipped all of our waiters, who were marvelous the whole time we were on the ship. So, too, was the dining experience-seven-course meals were the norm. After dinner we attended "Cabaret Showtime and the "Talent Show." Finally, we attended the midnight buffet. You know how in the movies when there's a scene on a cruise ship, you always see the couple out on the deck late at night and the moon is shining so brightly and everything is so romantic? Our late strolls weren't like that-it was almost always rainy, windy and cold. The setting wasn't so romantic for us.

So…

We made it romantic. We ran outside real quickly, kissed and hugged each other, and then ran back inside. The ship was really rocking that night after we got to bed.

Our cabin attendants could not speak English, so we did a lot of sign language. That last day we found out one could speak German. That might have come in handy, knowing that earlier.

On Saturday, July 13th, w got up at 5 a.m. so we could see the ship come into Vancouver. Breakfast was at 6:30. After breakfast we cleared out our room and waited to be called for check-out. We were checked out with the yellow #1 tag. We left the ship at about 10:30, and, of course, it was raining. We watched our luggage come off the ship. How it survives is a wonder. We said goodbye to our friends and departed. Each of us went our ways. Alvin and I took a but to the Vancouver airport to catch our Delta flight to Los Angeles. We changed planes there and headed to DFW International. Gene and Mark Johnson picked us up at 11 p.m.

Our tour cost us $1,589 each. This included airfare to Anchorage, our cruise and airfare to Dallas. This was the first cruise that I had ever been on. Alvin and I really enjoyed it.

# *Epilogue*

This book, which serves as my heartfelt tribute to Gracie, concludes with her simple yet profound words, "I really enjoyed it." Although she was referring to our unforgettable trip to Alaska, those words encapsulate so much more than just a moment in time; they represent the essence of our shared life together.

Gracie demonstrated her ability to wholeheartedly enjoy life's experiences throughout her lifetime. She infused every aspect of our life with an infectious energy, whether we were exploring new places or enjoying evenings at home.

Gracie possessed an extraordinary talent to find beauty in ordinary things while discovering magic in daily life which led others to stop and appreciate the momentary wonders of existence. Her positive view of life transformed our shared journey into an intricate tapestry filled with love and laughter alongside mutual dreams. My appreciation for the sunsets we watched and the shared meals and adventures we took grew through her perspective.

Looking back at our shared years fills me with profound thankfulness. Gracie's joy served as my life's guiding light because it gave me meaningful purpose which I struggle to put into words. The happiness she possessed created waves that reached our families and friends and touched every person in our network. Gracie's genuine happiness makes my life complete and deeply meaningful.

The pages of our life together bring back memories of her brilliant smile and constant support as well as her comforting embrace. Our shared journeys and memories stand as a testament to a love which remains permanently recorded in my heart. When I reflect on our shared life I recognize the importance of both celebrating our good times and honoring the difficulties that helped to shape who we became. Side by side we confronted every challenge because our shared love strengthened us and we became stronger together.

The conclusion of this book brings me a renewed sense of hope and an enduring feeling of continuity. Every written word carries Gracie's spirit which demonstrates how love extends beyond our physical moments together. In my memories her laughter fills the air with joy which remains an inspiration and her zest for life gives me strength to move forward.

I conclude this chapter with a joyful spirit because Gracie taught me to welcome life with open arms. Her words serve as a reminder that happiness exists within the smallest experiences. I want to memorialize her legacy through my own life filled with enthusiasm and gratitude as she demonstrated while embracing life's beauty and pleasures.

www.ingramcontent.com/pod-product-compliance
Lightning Source LLC
Chambersburg PA
CBHW051224120626
46547CB00013B/1491